TECHNICAL REPORT

Views from the Homefront

The Experiences of Youth and Spouses from Military Families

Anita Chandra • Sandraluz Lara-Cinisomo • Lisa H. Jaycox • Terri Tanielian
Bing Han • Rachel M. Burns • Teague Ruder

Sponsored by the National Military Family Association, with
funding from the Robertson Foundation and the Sierra Club Foundation

RAND Center for Military Health Policy Research

A JOINT ENDEAVOR OF RAND HEALTH AND THE
RAND NATIONAL SECURITY RESEARCH DIVISION

The research described in this report was sponsored by the National Military Family Association, with funding from the Robertson Foundation and the Sierra Club Foundation. The research was conducted jointly by RAND Health's Center for Military Health Policy Research and the Forces and Resources Policy Center of the RAND National Security Research Division.

Library of Congress Cataloging-in-Publication Data

Views from the homefront : the experiences of youth and spouses from military families / Anita Chandra ... [et al.].
p. ; cm.
Includes bibliographical references.
ISBN 978-0-8330-5127-1 (pbk. : alk. paper)
1. Children of military personnel. I. Chandra, Anita.
[DNLM: 1. Family Relations. 2. Adolescent. 3. Anxiety, Separation. 4. Child. 5. Military Personnel. 6. Stress, Psychological. WS 105.5.F2]

UB403.V54 2011
355.1'20973—dc22

2010047953

The RAND Corporation is a nonprofit institution that helps improve policy and decisionmaking through research and analysis. RAND's publications do not necessarily reflect the opinions of its research clients and sponsors.

Published 2011 by the RAND Corporation
1776 Main Street, P.O. Box 2138, Santa Monica, CA 90407-2138
1200 South Hayes Street, Arlington, VA 22202-5050
4570 Fifth Avenue, Suite 600, Pittsburgh, PA 15213-2665
RAND URL: http://www.rand.org/
To order RAND documents or to obtain additional information, contact
Distribution Services: Telephone: (310) 451-7002;
Fax: (310) 451-6915; Email: order@rand.org

Preface

As the United States continues deployments of service members to support operations in Iraq and Afghanistan, it is increasingly important to understand the effects of this military involvement, not only on service members but also on the health and well-being of their spouses and children. The purpose of this report is to examine the functioning of a sample of youth in military families who applied to the *Operation Purple®* camp program in the context of the current deployments and to specifically assess how they and their nondeployed caregivers are coping with parental deployment. In addition, the study addresses the relative dearth of information on the general well-being of military youth, with attention to their emotional, social, and academic functioning. The findings should be of interest to policymakers in the Department of Defense as well as those in the nongovernmental sector who fund, oversee, or deliver support to military families.

This research was sponsored by the National Military Family Association, with funding from the Robertson Foundation and the Sierra Club Foundation, and conducted jointly by RAND Health's Center for Military Health Policy Research and the Forces and Resources Policy Center of the RAND National Security Research Division (NSRD). The Center for Military Health Policy Research taps RAND expertise in both defense and health policy to conduct research for the Department of Defense, the Veterans Administration, and nonprofit organizations. RAND Health aims to transform the well-being of all people by solving complex problems in health and health care. NSRD conducts research and analysis on defense and national security topics for the U.S. and allied defense, foreign policy, homeland security, and intelligence communities and foundations and other nongovernmental organizations that support defense and national security analysis.

For more information on the Center for Military Health Policy Research, see http://www.rand.org/multi/military/ or contact the co-directors, Terri Tanielian or Susan Hosek (contact information is provided on the web page). For more information on the Forces and Resources Policy Center, see http://www.rand.org/nsrd/about/frp.html or contact the director, James Hosek (contact information is provided on the web page).

Contents

Figures

Tables

Summary

Background: Focus on Military Families

The wars in Iraq and Afghanistan represent the largest stress on the all-volunteer force since its inception in the early 1970s. Since late 2001, the United States has deployed approximately 2 million service members to support these operations. The pace of these deployments has been frequent, with many service members deploying several times over the past nine years, often with little quality time at home in between deployments. These deployments have also engaged the National Guard and Reserve forces extensively. In theater, the nature of combat exposure has placed additional stress on service members. Given the use of improvised explosive devices and the various insurgencies, there is no real front line. As such, even those in support roles are exposed to combat-related stressors.

The stressors that service members face during deployment may also influence the experiences of family members, both during the deployment and after the return home. However, the impact of these unique deployments and the wartime environment on military families is still not well understood.

A small but growing body of research has examined the impact of deployment on military families and has yielded valuable insights. However, there has been relatively little work in several areas: First, there is little information on how youth (and specifically pre-teens and teenagers) are faring across multiple domains or on understanding the experiences of youth as informed by both their own and adult perspectives. Second, there are few data on the challenges specifically related to deployment and reintegration that military youth face and how these challenges may differ by factors, such as youth age or gender, family military service or component, or the family's military deployment history, including number of deployments and total months of deployment. Finally, there has been relatively little analysis of how the wartime environment and deployments affect the emotional and psychological well-being of the spouse or other caregiver who stays at home to care for the family.

Study Purpose and Approach

This study is intended to begin addressing these research gaps. It represents the first comprehensive (i.e., across multiple domains), longitudinal examination of the behavioral and emotional well-being of a select sample of military families as they cope with the stress of war and deployment. The aim of the study is not to summarize the experience of all military families but rather to describe perspectives of a sample of military youth applying to *Operation Purple*®, a summer camp program. The study addresses three research questions:

- How are military youth who applied to this summer camp program functioning emotionally, socially, and academically?
- What, if any, challenges do these study participants report during and after parental deployment?
- How are their nondeployed caregivers faring, particularly related to deployment?

To address these questions, a team of RAND researchers surveyed and interviewed a sample of military families from among the applicants to the 2008 *Operation Purple*® camp, a free camp for children from military families that is sponsored by the National Military Family Association. There are camps at 63 sites nationwide. Children between ages 7 and 17 can attend, and multiple children from one family are eligible for the camps. The mission of *Operation Purple*® is to help children meet other military youth and for those who have experienced a parental deployment to cope with the stress of war.

Initially, we recruited 1,507 youth aged 11–17 years from the *Operation Purple*® applicant pool to participate in our study. We attempted to minimize some issues of selection bias by randomly selecting from the *Operation Purple*® applicants to include families that mirrored the service and component composition of deploying personnel in November 2007 (the most current data at the time of the study). However, since applicants to *Operation Purple*® are a service-seeking or program-seeking population of military families, we place study findings in this context throughout the report.

The study had two components: quantitative and qualitative. The quantitative component consisted of phone surveys with one youth and his or her nondeployed or "home" caregiver from each of the participating families at three time points over the course of one year: baseline in the summer of 2008, six months later in the winter of 2009, and then one year later in the summer of 2009. The surveys included the same questions to allow for repeated measurement across time, with the exception of open-ended questions about deployment experience that changed wave to wave. The second, qualitative, component involved in-depth, semistructured phone interviews with nondeployed caregivers to provide additional detail on how parental deployment affected family life and the experiences of the nondeployed caregiver.

We applied a set of general linear mixed models (McCulloch and Searle, 2001) to estimate the relationship between the outcomes of interest and key predictors while accounting for relevant covariates. We primarily used the longitudinal data set to explore which factors were significantly associated with outcomes of interest throughout the study period, rather than at a single point in time. We also examined whether there were any notable trends in how functioning (well-being) and the experience of deployment-related challenges changed over the study period, particularly for those who had experienced a deployment at baseline or during the study period and/or the return of a deployed parent during the study period. Our qualitative analysis employed traditional inductive coding processes to identify salient themes related to how nondeployed caregivers cope with parental deployment.

Key Findings

Below we summarize our findings for each of the research questions.

Youth Functioning and Well-Being

Using reports from both youth and their caregivers, we examined youth functioning and well-being in five areas: emotional difficulties, anxiety symptoms, peer and family functioning, academic engagement problems, and risk behaviors. For purposes of comparison, we used population-based data from studies of national samples of U.S. youth from the same age group, to the extent that those data were available.

Emotional or Behavioral Difficulties. We found that youth in our study were experiencing relatively high levels of emotional or behavioral difficulties. Overall, 30 percent of caregivers in the study at baseline reported moderate-to-high levels of emotional or behavioral difficulties among their children. At the 6-month and 12-month interviews, caregiver reports of youth difficulties decreased on average (compared with what these average scores were at baseline), but nearly 30 percent of caregivers in the study still reported difficulties in the moderate-to-high range. Among caregivers of youth 11–14 years, 34 percent in our study sample reported elevated emotional or behavioral problems compared with only 19 percent of youth this age in the general population.

Youth in the study also reported on their emotional or behavioral difficulties. Approximately 44 percent of youth in the study reported difficulties in the moderate-to-high range at baseline; this dropped to an average of 38 percent at 6 and 12 months.

Anxiety Symptoms. We found that youth in our study sample reported experiencing anxiety symptoms at levels that were higher than the average observed in other studies of youth. Thirty percent of the youth in our study reported elevated anxiety symptom levels, compared with 15 percent of youth in civilian studies. Over the study period (or survey wave to wave), anxiety symptoms reported by study participants decreased overall on average.

Peer and Family Functioning. Among our sample at baseline, caregiver reports of youth peer functioning problems were comparable to levels found in studies of other U.S. youth, but family functioning problems were slightly worse. Over the study year, peer functioning improved slightly; family functioning issues remained unchanged on average.

Academic Engagement Problems. We queried study participants about their ability to attend to tasks at school. Overall, report of academic issues was comparable to other studies of U.S. youth. Over the study period, youth academic engagement changed. On average, the score improved significantly between the 6-month and 12-month surveys.

Risk Behaviors. We asked youth in our study sample about their engagement in problem or risk behaviors, such as getting into fights with peers, getting into trouble at school, and using alcohol or other substances. Overall, study youth reported problem behaviors at rates comparable to those in other U.S. studies. For the purpose of this analysis, we compared only groups of youth on those items that all respondents answered, regardless of age. Over the study year, there was no change in the levels of youth-reported risk behaviors.

Groups Reporting More Problems in Functioning and Well-Being. The longitudinal data analyses identified particular subgroups and factors that were associated with greater levels of problems in functioning and well-being in our study sample.

- Older teens in our study reported more difficulties academically, while younger teens reported more anxiety symptoms.
- Girls in our study reported more anxiety symptoms.
- Caregivers in our study who were faring well emotionally were more likely to have children who were functioning well.
- Youth–caregiver communication problems were associated with youth functioning difficulties.

Deployment-Related Issues for Youth

The research team also examined issues for youth specifically related to parental deployment and reintegration using two scales for measuring deployment and reintegration challenges, one each for the caregiver and youth reports.

Deployment-Related Challenges. During a deployment, youth in our study sample reported that *dealing with life without the deployed parent* (68 percent) and *helping the caregiver deal with life without deployed parent* (68 percent) were the most difficult. Another frequently endorsed concern was *not having people in the community understand what deployment is like* (45 percent).

We also asked caregivers about youth difficulties during deployment. Caregivers in our study endorsed two items as the most difficult challenges for their child during deployment: *dealing with life without the deployed parent* (72 percent) and *feeling overwhelmed by new responsibilities at home* (57 percent).

Reintegration Challenges. We also asked youth and caregivers about reintegration challenges. Youth in our study cited two challenges most frequently: *fitting returning parent back into home routine* (54 percent) and *worrying about the next deployment* (47 percent). Caregivers in our study cited the same item as the most difficult challenge for their child during reintegration—*fitting the returning parent back into the home routine* (62 percent). Caregivers cited *getting to know the deployed parent again* (52 percent) as the second most difficult challenge.

Groups Reporting More Deployment and Reintegration Challenges. The longitudinal analysis identified subgroups in our study sample who had more problems over the course of the study year that were specifically related to deployment or reintegration:

- Older teens, youth experiencing more cumulative months of parental deployment, and youth whose caregiver had poorer emotional well-being reported more difficulties during deployment.
- Girls in the study reported more difficulties related to reintegration.
- Caregivers in the study with spouses in the Reserve component (Guard or Reserve) were more likely to report that their children faced deployment and reintegration challenges.

Caregiver Well-Being

We also asked caregivers in the study about their own well-being. With respect to caregiver well-being, we asked about their emotional status, as well as issues related to household management, their relationship with the deployed parent, and parenting issues. These are all areas in which significant changes may occur during a deployment. We then asked caregivers about challenges specifically related to the period of deployment.

Caregiver Emotional Well-Being. We assessed the emotional well-being of caregivers. We found that, within our sample and on average, caregivers' emotional well-being improved over the study period, although there were important variations among subgroups, as we describe below. Decreases in difficulties between baseline and 6 months were not significant, but improvement in well-being between baseline and 12 months was marginally significant.

Household Hassles. A deployment may translate into loss of emotional or other kinds of support for caregivers, which may, in turn, lead to increased household burdens. We queried caregivers about the degree to which household-related challenges bothered them. Caregivers in the study were most bothered by the following household hassle at baseline: *not having time to do things they wanted to do* (53 percent) and *having too many responsibilities at home* (47 percent). The average report of household hassles declined over the course of the study.

Relationship Hassles. Prior research suggests that deployment can have a negative impact on the relationship between the caregiver and the deployed service member. The most frequently endorsed relationship hassles among our study sample at baseline were *changing roles in the marriage* (30 percent) and *problems growing apart from the partner* (25 percent). The average number of relationship hassles reported increased slightly from wave to wave over the study period.

Parenting Hassles. Caregivers were asked about a range of parenting challenges they had experienced in the six months prior to the interview, such as challenges related to parenting the focal child. Of these, concerns about *child's behavior in school* (42 percent) and *problems with child's behavior* (31 percent) most bothered caregivers in the study. The average report of parenting hassles decreased over the course of the study year.

Groups of Caregivers and Factors Associated with Well-Being Problems. We found that certain caregiver groups in the study reported more difficulties with well-being. We also found that certain factors were associated with more problems.

- Reserve component caregivers in the study reported poorer emotional well-being and higher numbers of household challenges.
- Household challenges decreased for families in the study as the quality of family communication increased on average wave to wave.
- Reserve component caregivers and all caregivers facing a current deployment in the study reported a higher number of relationship issues.
- Parenting issues were greater for caregivers of boys and those experiencing a deployment at the time of the study.
- Caregiver emotional well-being was the most salient variable across all challenges, with poorer emotional well-being associated with more challenges.

Caregiver Challenges Specifically Related to Deployment

The study team created scales to measure caregiver challenges specifically related to deployment and reintegration.

Key deployment challenges for caregivers in the study were the following: *taking on more responsibilities at home caring for children* (83 percent) and *helping child deal with life without the deployed parent* (80 percent). Difficulties reported did not change significantly during the study period.

During reintegration, the most widely cited caregiver challenges were *fitting deployed parent back into the home routine* (71 percent) and *rebalancing childcare responsibilities* (61 percent). Difficulties reported did not change significantly during the study period.

Conclusions

In interpreting our findings and drawing conclusions from them, it is important to bear in mind the unique characteristics of our study sample, which consisted of self-selected military families who were seeking a program. In particular, it should be noted that families in our study may have been experiencing more difficulties at the time of their application to *Operation Purple®* than other military families, thus overestimating need. In the clinical services literature, those who are service-seeking tend to have higher need than the general population. On the other hand, these study families may also have access to resources that other families lack. In the youth development field, those young people who are at higher risk are the most difficult to recruit into programs. Thus, the absolute level of problems may be an underestimate relative to families who are in more distress and unable to organize to gain access to programs like *Operation Purple®*. Regardless of which (if any) of these presumptive explanations is true, we were able to identify which subgroups of families experienced relatively more or fewer difficulties. Doing so will help improve efforts to align program content more accurately with the needs of those seeking services.

Keeping this in mind, we conclude the following: Children and nondeployed caregivers who had applied to *Operation Purple®* confronted significant challenges to their emotional well-being and functioning. Four factors in particular—(1) caregiver emotional well-being, (2) more cumulative months of deployment, (3) National Guard or Reserve status, and (4) quality of caregiver-youth communication—were strongly associated with greater youth or caregiver difficulties. We discuss each of these factors in more detail below.

- *Caregiver emotional well-being.* Among the study sample, we found that caregiver emotional well-being is related to both the caregiver and the youth across a number of dimensions. Caregivers in the study who reported poorer emotional well-being also reported that their children had greater emotional, social, and academic difficulties. Further, if caregiver emotional health difficulties persisted or increased on average over the study period, youth difficulties remained higher when compared with youth whose caregivers reported fewer emotional difficulties. Lower levels of caregiver emotional well-being were also associated with greater stressors for the caregiver, including more challenges maintaining the household, parenting, and relating to the deployed parent.
- *More cumulative months of deployment.* Families in the study that experienced more total months of parental deployment also reported more youth emotional difficulties, and these difficulties did not diminish over the study period. Families in the study with more months of deployment reported more problems both during deployment and reintegration.
- *National Guard and Reserve status.* Caregivers in the study with partners in the Reserve component (Guard or Reserves) reported more challenges than their counterparts in the Active component. In particular, Guard and Reserve caregivers in the study reported more difficulties with emotional well-being, as well as more challenges during and after deployment.

- *Quality of caregiver-youth communication.* The quality of communication between caregivers and their children was highly associated with family functioning. In addition, the quality of family communication indicated how well families were functioning. Families in the study reporting poorer youth–caregiver communication also reported more problems with youth well-being.

In addition, the study identified challenges specifically related to the deployment and reintegration of a parent/spouse.

- A major challenge during deployment was difficulties maintaining the household. Across the study period, we noted that both caregivers and youth in the study cited difficulties with taking on more household responsibilities. For caregivers, this included more parenting responsibilities, and for youth this included taking care of siblings. In addition, both caregivers and youth in the study reported difficulties confronting life without the deployed parent. Youth and caregivers also reported difficulties during deployment due to what they perceived as a lack of community understanding of what life was like for them during this period. This was particularly an issue for caregivers from the Reserve component.
- Caregivers and youth in the study noted that reintegration of the deployed parent, while a joyous experience, also brought readjustment challenges. Caregivers described difficulties in rebalancing childcare responsibilities while still ensuring that the deployed parent had the necessary time to adjust to home life. Youth in the study, on the other hand, did not experience this type of improvement if their parent returned, although it is possible that such improvement may occur but take longer to observe. Youth also reported that understanding their deployed parent again, particularly if that parent experienced mood changes, was difficult.

Recommendations

Based on these findings, we offer the following recommendations for policy and programmatic action, as well as further research.

- **Review availability of support programs or services, including mental health services, for caregivers.**

Given the importance of caregiver emotional well-being as a factor related to youth well-being, ensuring the availability of and access to mental health services for spouses and children is important. In addition, more social and instrumental support services may be warranted. Caregivers have more responsibilities to juggle and thus may require help to balance these new burdens. Programs to help caregivers anticipate and plan for these changes may also be helpful. In addition, programs to help caregivers develop and maintain healthy social support networks, including those with other military spouses, may mitigate some of these stressors.

- **Target support for those families reporting children with elevated emotional difficulties and experiencing more months of deployment.**

We noted that some youth in the study reported greater emotional difficulties or elevated anxiety symptoms during the study period, signifying that certain youth may be struggling with problems that do not diminish with time. As of this writing, military organizations do not have a systematic plan for screening and serving youth whose caregivers are experiencing significant months of deployment. Our findings also suggest that older teens (ages 15–17) and girls in particular may benefit from targeted initiatives.

- **Provide sufficient resources for caregiver support, particularly for Guard and Reserve caregivers.**

Our study findings show that Guard and Reserve caregivers in our study sample reported higher levels of difficulties. This finding should be interpreted in the context of the study's *Operation Purple®* applicant sample. Given that it can be challenging for Guard and Reserve families to link to services (e.g., due to lack of proximity to military installation or connection to military resources), our sample of Guard and Reserve families may represent a unique group who may have a greater ability to access resources. The fact that this group reports difficulties represents an opportunity to better serve this subgroup. For instance, we should examine the availability of formal and informal mental health services, particularly when families are geographically far from military mental health providers.

- **Focus programs on the quality of family communication.**

The quality of communication between caregivers and their children was associated with how families in the study fared during and after deployment. Thus, it is important to consider integrating evidence-based strategies in programs to improve the quality of caregiver–youth and caregiver–deployed parent communication. This may entail pre- and postdeployment interventions that address whole-family communication, focused on improving perceived empathy for each family member's experience.

- **Implement support programs across the deployment cycle, including during the reintegration period.**

We noted that families in the study faced challenges during deployment and reintegration, suggesting that support programs must be in place across the entire deployment cycle. Given the strong association between cumulative months of deployment and youth and caregiver difficulties, targeted initiatives for families experiencing many months of deployment may be needed.

In addition to these recommendations that specifically correspond to key subgroups reporting more challenges, the next two suggestions relate to the study findings as a whole.

- **Consider screening for family emotional well-being.**

Our examination of the well-being of youth and nondeployed caregivers suggests that some type of ongoing assessment of family member health and well-being before and after a deployment may be warranted.

- **Require evaluation of programs in light of existing research.**

Over the past seven years, there has been a rapid proliferation of programs to support military families. A rigorous and systematic evaluation of these programs is needed, including an assessment of how well program content aligns with the needs of the subgroups that would benefit most.

In addition, research needs to continue addressing gaps in understanding of the effects of deployment in youth and caregivers. In particular, there are four types of studies that are needed most urgently.

1. **Compare military families to civilian cohorts.** It is critical to understand how a contemporary cohort of youth is faring in order to isolate the unique stress that deployment may contribute. Future studies of this nature should consider including appropriately matched samples of nondeploying civilian youth. As with most studies to date of military youth, our sample had the limitations of convenience, in this case a population applying to a specialized summer camp program. Future efforts should use a population-based, representative sample.
2. **Examine caregiver well-being, with more measures of mental health.** Given the salience of caregiver emotional well-being, further examination of the mental health and well-being of caregivers is warranted, using validated mental health screening tools. To date, we have had limited information on the mental health of the caregivers.
3. **Tie longitudinal study periods to deployment periods.** A study that anchors all families to a deployment period to allow assessment before a deployment would improve measurement of the effects associated specifically with deployment, because there would be a common exposure point and all families could be examined on the same timeline.
4. **Follow youth over a longer period, into adulthood.** Following youth over a longer time period will help to determine if the emotional difficulties we noted in this study worsen across time points as deployments continue or level off. Tracking these youth into adulthood will also provide an opportunity to assess whether deployment-related challenges have an impact after adolescence.

Despite this need for additional research, the present study is able to provide important information about the status and experiences of a group of military families that are applying to *Operation Purple*®, a summer program designed specifically for military youth experiencing parental deployment. This gives insight into the large group of families interested in such types of services and answers questions about the extent of their difficulties.

Final Observation

The unique features of the current conflicts in Afghanistan and Iraq—including multiple, extended deployments—are creating psychological and emotional challenges for both service members and their families. This research represents an important first step in understanding the nature of those challenges for military youth and their nondeployed caregivers within a self-selected sample of military families that sought support services. The findings identified key factors that were related to the experience of greater challenge for behavioral and emotional difficulties and explores the potential consequences of these difficulties. Continuing to broaden and deepen understanding of the challenges facing military families by studying other samples of military youth, the challenges they face, and the resiliency resources they draw on in response will be critical for helping military organizations to understand their needs and to respond appropriately.

Acknowledgments

We extend our sincere appreciation to the National Military Family Association for sponsoring this research, with funding from the Robertson Foundation and the Sierra Club Foundation. In particular, we thank Patricia Montes Barron, Kelly Hruska, and Joyce Wessel Raezer for their collaboration. We are appreciative of Abt-SRBI, and Robert Magaw and Lisa Currie, in particular, for their assistance with data collection. We also thank Beth Asch, David Adamson, Susan Hosek, James Hosek, Rajeev Ramchand, Bonnie Ghosh Dastidar, and Terry Schell at RAND for their review of our research. Most importantly, we thank the families that participated in this study for their insight and willingness to share their experiences.

Abbreviations

APA	American Psychological Association
CATI	computer assisted telephone interview
CI	confidence interval
DP	deployed parent
HCG	home caregiver
MHI-5	5-item Mental Health Index
MI	multiple imputation
OEF	Operation Enduring Freedom
OIF	Operation Iraqi Freedom
OR	odds ratio
PBFS	Problem Behavior Frequency Scale
PedsQL	Pediatric Quality of Life Inventory
SCARED	Screen for Child Anxiety Related Emotional Disorders
SD	standard deviation
SDQ	Strengths and Difficulties Questionnaire
TDAP	Teen Depression Awareness Project

CHAPTER ONE

Introduction

The wars in Iraq and Afghanistan represent the largest stress on the all-volunteer force since its inception in the early 1970s. Since late 2001, the United States has deployed approximately 2 million service members to support these operations. The pace of these deployments has quickened, with many service members deploying several times over the past nine years, often with little quality time at home in between deployments. These deployments have also engaged the National Guard and Reserve forces extensively, a role which they have not played since World War II (Wormuth et al., 2006). Finally, given the use of improvised explosive devices and the various insurgencies experienced in both Iraq and Afghanistan, there is no real front line in today's wars. As such, even those in support roles are exposed to combat. Prior research has shown that even deployed units that are not exposed to direct combat may experience stressors that include strenuous training activities and physical challenges, long working hours and an intense working pace, infrequent breaks and little time off, close quarters and a lack of privacy, extreme environmental conditions, uncertainty and exposure to danger, and separation from family and friends (Hosek, Kavanagh, and Miller, 2006). Many service members also experience intense trauma, such as witnessing injury or death of friends and/or noncombatants, hand-to-hand combat, explosions and resulting blast injuries, and exposure to decomposing bodies (Tanielian et al., 2008; Hoge et al., 2004). Additionally, deployment-related stress is not limited just to those service members that deploy. Prior research also indicates that service members who do not deploy face stress as a result of increased workload and responsibilities (Hosek, Kavanagh, and Miller, 2006) during this period of high operational tempo for our forces.

The pace, frequency, and length of these deployments have also posed challenges for military families. It is well known that the stressors that service members face during deployment may also influence the experience of their family members, both during the deployment and after the return home. However, the impact of these current deployments on military families is still not well understood.

An Emerging Body of Research Focuses on Deployment and Children

Most research on the effects of deployment on behavioral and emotional well-being has focused, understandably, on military service members themselves. However, there are a growing number of studies examining the effects of deployment on military families.[1]

[1] A full literature review examining the effects of deployment associated with child and caregiver well-being is presented elsewhere (Chandra et al., 2008; 2011). We briefly summarize key findings from this review in the next few sections.

Studies Prior to Operations Enduring Freedom and Iraqi Freedom (OEF/OIF)

Research conducted prior to OEF and OIF and Desert Shield suggests an association between military parent separation and children's behavior, including increased aggressiveness and behavior problems, particularly among boys (Hillenbrand, 1976; Yeatman, 1981). Several pre-OEF/OIF studies of children of deployed parents (including deployments to Operation Desert Storm) indicated that deployment was associated with higher levels of internalizing behaviors, such as feeling sad, fearful, or over-controlled (Jensen et al., 1989; Levai et al., 1995; Jensen, Martin, and Watanabe, 1996). For example, Jensen and colleagues studied children of U.S. Army officers and senior enlisted personnel and found that children with absent fathers had significantly higher levels of depressive symptoms and anxiety than those children whose fathers were present; length of absence but not total number of absences was correlated with child-reported symptoms of depression and anxiety (Jensen et al., 1989).

OEF/OIF Studies

Since 2001, studies examining the effects of OEF and OIF deployments associated with child well-being have grown in number. These studies have shown increases in stress levels, increases in reports of child maltreatment by caregivers, and increases in school-related difficulties among children of deployed service members. With the exception of work by Huebner and Mancini (2005) and Chandra et al. (2008, 2010a, 2011), most of the research has focused on children age 12 and younger. For example, a study of children ages 5–12 found that those with deployed parents had mental health and behavioral problems at rates significantly higher than the national average (Flake et al., 2009). Barker and Berry (2009) found that children age 5 and under displayed increased behaviorial problems during deployment and increased attachment behaviors at reunion compared with children whose parents had not experienced a recent deployment; these attachment behaviors were related to length of deployment, number of deployments, and the number of stressors faced by the parent. Recent studies also suggest that child maltreatment and neglect may also increase during parental deployment (Gibbs et al., 2007). Huebner and Mancini (2005) found that teens reported changes in the relationship with the deployed parent, concern and anxiety about the deployed parent's well-being, increases in responsibility and demonstrations of maturity in caring for younger siblings and completing household chores, bonding with younger siblings, changes in daily routine due to transportation or financial reasons, and worse performance in school. Lester and colleagues (2010) interviewed children of active-duty Army and Marine Corps parents and found that anxiety levels were significantly elevated in children whose parents were currently deployed or recently returned compared with a community sample. Lipari et al. (2010) used data from the *2008 Active Duty Spouse Survey* and found that military spouses reported that their children exhibited an increase in problem behaviors following the first or second parental deployment but that those spouses experiencing a third deployment reported less problematic behavior among their children, possibly due to the development of coping strategies. In a survey of Army teens, Wong and Gerras (2010) found that the majority of respondents reported an ability to cope well with deployment. Those who reported the least stress also reported more supportive family environments, high activity (e.g., after-school and school participation), and a belief in the war and community support of the Army.

The few studies that have examined academic functioning among military children found that both reading and math scores were lower during parental deployment (Pisano, 1996; Lyle, 2006). Engel, Gallagher, and Lyle (2006) examined standardized test scores for 56,000 children in schools run by the Department of Defense between 2002 and 2005, and found that parental deployment was associated with lower test scores, especially in cases where the parent was deployed during the testing month. A recent study of school staff perspectives on student academic impact (Chandra et al., 2010b) revealed that teachers and counselors of military youth reported that the stress of deployment had a negative effect on student academic engagement. According to those teachers and counselors, while many military children were coping well with deployment, other youth were struggling with attendance, homework completion, and general engagement and participation in classroom activities. In addition, school staff in the study shared that some students had expressed stress that resulted in school behavioral issues and ultimately affected school performance.

Research on Deployment and Spouses Shows Some Negative Effects

Over the past several years, a small number of studies has explored how deployment is experienced by the nondeployed spouse or caregiver.

Pre-OEF/OIF Studies

Studies conducted prior to the pre-OEF/OIF conflicts present mixed findings. Most found some association between deployment and marital issues. In general, the separation of deployment was associated with diminished social support and poorer psychological well-being of the spouse (Raschmann, Patterson, and Schofield, 1989; Hiew, 1992; Burrell et al., 2006). However, a few studies found little or no deployment effect. A study of Navy families observed no significant effect of deployment on spousal well-being (Nice, 1981). Schumm, Bell, and Gade (2000) found that impending deployment was associated with marital discord, but after deployment for a peacekeeping mission, self-reported marital quality was not affected.

Combat Deployments

Most of the earlier studies on military spouses were conducted during peacekeeping operations rather than during deployments to support combat operations. Only a small number of studies focused on the effects of combat-related deployments, and these, too, have shown mixed results. Some studies have found that military combat deployment is related to spousal problems, including higher levels of depression and higher divorce rates (Jensen, Martin, and Watanabe, 1996; Angrist and Johnson, 2000; McCarroll et al., 2000). However, Schumm and colleagues (1996a) found that deployment during Operation Desert Storm was not associated with a significant change in self-reported marital satisfaction among active duty service members. Similarly, Schumm and colleagues (1996b) found that among enlisted soldiers deployed to Somalia for Operation Restore Hope and their civilian wives, stress during the deployment was not a predictor of marital dissatisfaction. These studies suggest a possible association between combat-related deployments and a negative impact on spouses; however, the results are inconsistent. In addition, the studies have methodological problems. The majority were cross-sectional, limiting the capability to attribute causality. In addition, not all studies control for predeployment (or premilitary) marital quality and/or spousal well-being. For example, we do not know if deployment exacerbates preexisting marital issues or causes new problems.

OEF/OIF Studies

While the number of studies focusing on the effects of OEF/OIF deployments is limited, results suggest that length of deployment is associated with declining spousal mental health (Mansfield et al., 2010). Eaton and colleagues (2008) found that soldiers' spouses have mental health problems at rates similar to those of soldiers during deployments with OEF/OIF. The loss of emotional and instrumental social support from the service member during deployment may lead spouses to experience increased household burdens or hassles, such as more chores and responsibilities (Drummet, Coleman, and Cable, 2003; Tomforde, 2006; Castaneda et al., 2008; Chandra et al., 2008). Deployments associated with the current wars may also result in a decline in marital satisfaction (Karney and Crown, 2007).

Gaps Remain in the Research

Although prior studies have yielded valuable insights, gaps in our knowledge base remain. For example, there has been relatively little work done in several areas. There is little information on how youth (pre-teens and teenagers specifically) are faring academically, socially, and emotionally. Most studies have gathered data from only one perspective; as such, there have been no studies that examined the experiences of military youth that were informed by both youth and adult perspectives. At the same time, few studies have assessed both challenges specifically related to deployment and challenges faced during the parent's reintegration. Finally, there has been relatively little analysis of the well-being of nondeployed caregivers and the sources of their stress.

Addressing the Gap

The work described in this report addresses these gaps. This study was designed to examine the functioning and well-being of a sample of military youth and their nondeployed or home caregivers who applied to *Operation Purple®* (a summer camp program for military youth), and to describe the deployment-specific challenges these family members confront. The aim of this study is not to summarize the experience of all military families but rather to describe perspectives of a sample of military youth applying to a summer camp program. This work is guided by an empirically derived conceptual framework that identified factors that may be related to youth functioning (see Figure 1.1). For example, prior research has demonstrated that deployment-related experiences and variables related to military background and deployment context are related to youth functioning. Further, earlier research shows differences in internalizing and externalizing behavior by youth age and gender. Both of these factors are included in the conceptual framework employed here.

The remainder of the report is organized in four chapters. Chapter Two describes the study's objectives and methods for collecting and analyzing data from youth applicants to *Operation Purple®* and their caregivers. Next, we present findings, organized into two chapters, "The Experience of Military Youth in the Study Sample" and "The Experience of Caregivers in the Study Sample." The final chapter presents the study conclusions as well as recommendations for policy, program development, and research based on the analysis.

Figure 1.1
Proposed Relationship Between Individual/Family, Military, and Deployment Characteristics and Youth and Caregiver Outcomes

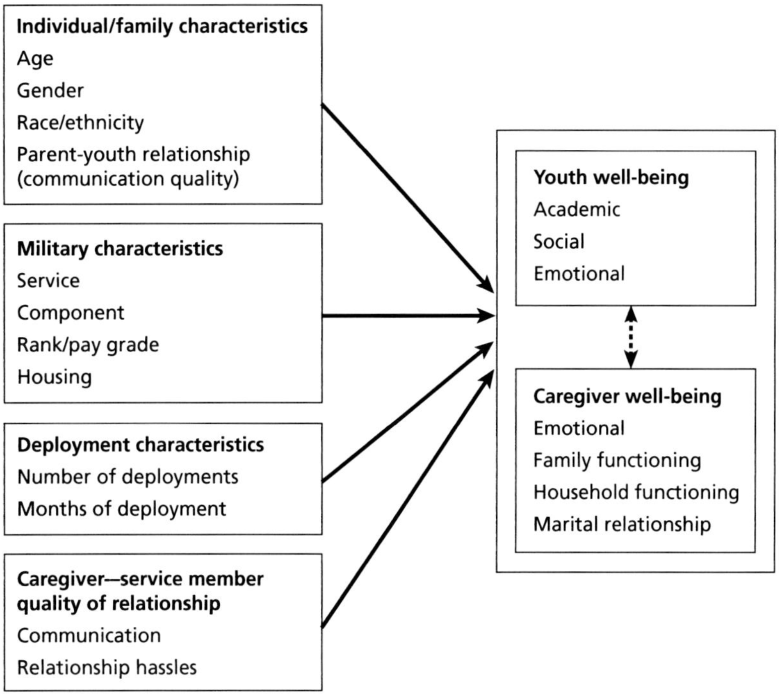

RAND *TR913-1.1*

CHAPTER TWO

Methods

In this chapter, we provide an overview of the study design and present detail about the study methods, including a discussion regarding the unique characteristics of the study sample. We provide information on the measures used in the study and then describe our approach to data analysis. First, we provide some context for the conduct of the study.

This Study Builds on an Earlier Exploratory Study

To begin to address some of the research gaps identified from prior studies, we conducted an exploratory study in 2007 (Summer 2007–Winter 2008) to describe the well-being of a sample of children of military personnel who attended *Operation Purple*®, along with their non-deployed caregivers. In this section, we briefly describe the study sample, design, and findings. Additional detail was published previously (Chandra et al., 2008).

Study Sample

For the pilot study, we drew the sample from *Operation Purple*®, a summer camp program sponsored by the National Military Family Association since 2004 to provide military children with an opportunity to meet other military children and to learn more about coping with deployment. The camps are offered in dozens of locations across the United States. Various organizations, such as the YMCA and camp grounds, offer their camp sites for one week each summer for *Operation Purple*®. Priority is usually provided to youth experiencing a current or impending parental deployment at the time of application.

Exploratory Study Design

We conducted a self-administered paper-and-pencil survey with approximately 192 families (two respondents per family, youth, and a nondeployed caregiver)—before and after attendance at an *Operation Purple*® camp and three months later. This was a convenience sample whereby we selected five camps conducted in the month of August and located on the East Coast (based on study start time and feasibility). The camps had a mix of participants by service and component (e.g., a camp in Pennsylvania was selected due to high National Guard participation). In the study, we assessed youth at three time points—baseline (before camp started), at the end of camp, and three months after camp concluded. We also surveyed caregivers at baseline and at three months following the end of camp. The eligible age range in the selected camps was 7–17 years.

Key Pilot Study Findings

Overall, caregivers for youth attending *Operation Purple®* reported levels of youth emotional and behavioral difficulties that were higher than those reported by parents/caregivers in the general population (U.S. Department of Health and Human Services, 2001). In addition, youth attending *Operation Purple®* and their caregivers described challenges of parental deployment that included a lack of community understanding about what deployment entails, difficulties in school, and problems handling new household responsibilities. Details of the study findings can be found in Chandra et al. (2008; 2011).

While this study offered important information on the well-being of youth and families and the impact of deployment, it was an exploratory effort based on a relatively small convenience sample. The work suggested that a larger sample with more families better distributed by military service (e.g., Army, Navy) and component (e.g., Active, Reserve) was needed. Following a larger sample would also allow for conducting analysis of subgroups to identify which groups of youth may report greater difficulties.

Approach to the Current Study

To address some of the methodological issues and limitations raised by the exploratory study, we pursued a second phase of the study that would continue to address the research gaps described in Chapter One. As described in Chapter One, the aim of the present study is not to summarize the experience of all military families but rather to describe perspectives of a sample of military youth applying to *Operation Purple®*. We designed a 12-month longitudinal study to answer three critical questions:

- How are military youth who applied to a summer camp program functioning emotionally, socially, and academically?
- What, if any, challenges do these study participants report during and after parental deployment?
- How are their nondeployed caregivers faring, particularly related to deployment?

For these research questions, we were primarily interested in understanding (1) whether certain subgroups of youth and nondeployed caregivers in the study sample reported more problems and (2) how different experiences with parental deployment (in the case of youth) and "other parent" deployment (in the case of nondeployed caregiver) may be associated with a differential experience of problems.

Study Design

This longitudinal study of *Operation Purple®* applicants consisted of two components that combined quantitative and qualitative approaches. The quantitative component entailed computer assisted telephone interviews (CATIs) with youth and caregivers from participating families at three time points over 12 months: The baseline was conducted during Summer 2008, with two follow-ups 6 months later in Winter 2009, and then 12 months later during Summer 2009. Caregivers were defined as the nondeployed primary caregiver who was responsible for taking care of the child when a parent was deployed, or the "home caregiver" (HCG). In this study, the nondeployed caregiver was most frequently the mother.

The second, qualitative component involved in-depth, semistructured phone interviews with a randomly selected subgroup of nondeployed caregivers from the first component. The study was approved by the RAND Human Subjects Protection Committee. Human subjects protection included providing all families with information about resources available to them (e.g., Military OneSource). This was not an intervention study, nor did the survey employ diagnostic questions.

Quantitative Component: Phone Surveys with Youth and Caregiver. We partnered with Abt-SRBI, a nationally recognized survey company with extensive research experience with military families, to conduct the CATI (or phone interviews) with one youth (11–17 years old) and caregiver. We included this age range for two reasons. First, we wanted the youth to be able to complete fairly lengthy (30–45 minute) surveys by phone. Second, some of the well-being assessment scales used in this study were valid for this age range, and we wanted to compare data for the study sample with other youth studies.

A complete caregiver and youth interview took approximately one hour. The general sequence was to screen the caregiver to describe the study, secure consent and permission to interview the youth, and conduct the HCG interview. This was followed by obtaining youth assent and conducting the youth interview. We conducted a pilot test of the instruments with an initial sample of families (n=20) to check if survey questions were confusing, and to determine study length. In order to reduce respondent burden, the final survey took approximately 30 minutes and the youth interview closer to 20 minutes. Interview break-offs were allowed, so that some interviews were completed in more than one call. Each interview included questions related to well-being and deployment experiences. Most questions were closed-ended (i.e., with fixed response options), with a few open-ended questions (i.e., free-form, text responses). Questions were repeated at each survey wave to allow for measurement with the same scales over the three time points. We also closely monitored the quality of interviews and received daily dispositions on participant enrollment from Abt-SRBI. Quality monitoring was conducted at each survey wave. Study team members were assigned to listening sessions during different days of the week and times of day to review a diverse set of interviewers. If there was a concern regarding interviewer quality, study team members provided that feedback in real time to the call center field monitor, and corrections were made. In addition, we conducted interviewer trainings before each survey wave to address any issues of question clarity.

Each participating family received an appreciation payment for completing each survey wave ($40, $45, and $50, for each survey wave, respectively), in the form of a check.

Qualitative Component: In-Depth Caregiver Interviews. The second component consisted of in-depth, qualitative interviews with a randomly selected sample of caregivers from the survey sample (n=50). The purpose of the qualitative component was to obtain greater insight into the deployment experience for caregivers, the types of stressors they confronted, and how they addressed or coped with these challenges. These interviews included questions about life changes for the caregiver during deployment and reintegration, including changes in household responsibilities, marital/partner relationship, and family relationships.

Those caregivers who also participated in the qualitative, in-depth interview component received a gift card in the amount of $25.

Study Sample

Sample Frame. Since there was no readily accessible roster of all military youth in the United States from which to sample, we drew the study sample from among the applicants to the 2008 *Operation Purple®* summer camp. To prepare for this study, the National Military Family Association, who runs the program and sponsored this study, included information about the potential for being selected for this study in their 2008 application materials. Applicants were asked to provide permission to share their information with RAND if they were randomly selected. As described earlier, *Operation Purple®* is a free camp sponsored by the National Military Family Association for children of military service members (ages 7–17) at 63 sites nationwide. The mission of *Operation Purple®* is to provide military children with an opportunity to meet other military children and to learn more about coping with deployment. Preference is given to those families experiencing a current or impending parental deployment at the time of application. Approximately 9,138 youth between the ages of 7 to 17 attended camp in 2008, with closer to 15,000 youth applying that spring. The National Military Family Association provided contact information for *Operation Purple®* applicants, including age, and we sampled youth between 11 and 17 years of age from that list for recruitment into the study. The sampling strategy is described in more detail below.

Although all youth study participants applied to *Operation Purple®* in the spring of 2008, they were not necessarily accepted to the camp and did not necessarily attend it in the summer of 2008 or the summer of 2009. Thus, attendance at camp is included in all relevant analytic models. In addition, although the *Operation Purple®* camps were geared toward families experiencing deployment, not all participating youth had parents deploy during the study period. Also, parents could deploy at different times and for different lengths of time. Thus, we carefully explored the deployment status of each family at each survey wave.

Sample Characteristics and Potential Limitations. The sample under study was drawn from the *Operation Purple®* applicant pool and thus is a subsample of military youth who were interested in attending a specialized, free summer program for military youth. During the baseline survey, we queried caregivers about the reasons that they applied to camp for their children. Reasons most frequently cited as "very important" included the following: *enjoy camp activities* (84.5 percent), *meet other military kids* (83.2 percent) and *make new friends* (73.3 percent). Less frequently cited reasons include *getting away from home* (26.6 percent), *giving caregivers a rest* (17.1 percent), and *giving the caregiver and spouse time together* (10.7 percent). While we purposely conducted disproportionate sampling by service and component in order for this sample to be better distributed by military service (e.g., Army, Navy) and component (e.g., Active, Reserve), these applicants may have been different from other military families by either having more difficulties (hence, needing the camp) or less difficulties (more organized, more knowledgeable or connected to military support in order to know to apply for the camp). Thus, the findings presented here may either overestimate or underestimate the extent of youth and caregiver challenges among all military youth. The clinical services literature suggests that those seeking services may be more in need than the general population; however, the youth development research also points to the difficulties of recruiting at-risk or higher-need youth into programs like summer camp (Lauver and Little, 2005; Noam, 2005).

Second, the study included only families with youth between the ages of 11 and 17. Thus, compared with military youth in general, participating families tended to have been in the military longer and to be made up of older parents who may have had greater access to and awareness of services like *Operation Purple®*, and perhaps greater ability to identify social and emotional needs in their children. It should be noted that the analytic models described in the next section did explore years in military service as a factor, but that factor was dropped from our final models since we did not observe any statistically significant relationships. Further, due to the age of the youth, we had very few families from the lower enlisted ranks (E1–E4) from which to draw our sample. We know from mental health research that low income or socioeconomic status (as related to lower enlisted rank) is associated with greater experience of stress and mental health difficulties (Andrade, 2000; Turner, 1999). Thus, our results should be interpreted with these factors in mind.

Throughout the analysis and conclusions (Chapters Three through Five), we use the context of the study sample to frame the study findings and identify what we may be able to assert about military youth and what may be uniquely related to a service-seeking population.

Eligibility. To determine eligibility for study participation, Abt-SRBI (the survey firm that conducted the phone surveys under contract to RAND) conducted a test to determine which phone numbers were valid (e.g., working numbers, not cell phones, etc.) (see Appendix A for study flow chart). Numerous families selected for participation had more than one youth that met the age criteria. In those cases, we randomly selected one youth to participate in the study (using the first letter of the youth's name). Over three thousand phone numbers were dialed (n=3,165), with the goal of enrolling 1,500 families to participate.

At baseline, we recruited 1,507 youth from the *Operation Purple®* applicant pool to participate in the study. We stratified the sample by service and component and then randomly selected the families to call within those strata. Our quotas were driven to mirror the composition of the deploying personnel as of November 2007 (the most current data at the time of the study) by service (Army, Navy, Air Force, Marines) and component (Active, Reserve). We included Coast Guard families in the initial recruitment, although the *Operation Purple®* applicant pool did not have enough from which to draw an adequate stratum for subsequent analysis.

Study Enrollment and Response Rates. As shown in Table 2.1, 89 percent of household screened agreed to participate. Table 2.1 also provides a count of the number who refused to participate after being read a description of the study. Table 2.1 also provides the number of households who were not eligible (n=49) and the number who participated in the study.

Of the 1,507 surveys administered, 97 percent were surveys completed by caregivers and youth (see Table 2.2). Caregivers were read a description about the caregiver and youth survey. At the time of enrollment, all 1,507 caregivers agreed to participate in the study and to allow their child to participate in the study. However, after completing the caregiver survey, 18 caregivers refused to allow their child to participate. Among those who allowed their child to participate, 13 children completed only a portion of the interview. In some of those cases, chil-

Table 2.1
Close to 90 Percent of Contacts Converted to Study Participation

	Screened Contacts (n=1,697)	
	Number from Total	**Percent from Total**
Total completed	1,507	89
Not eligible (e.g., No youth who applied to *Operation Purple®)*	49	3
Refusals	141	8

Table 2.2
Caregiver and Youth Completion Rates

	Completed Surveys (n=1,507)	
	Number from Total	**Percent of Total**
Caregiver and youth completed	1,456	97
Caregiver only/caregiver refused youth survey	18	1
Caregiver only/youth partial	13	1
Caregiver only/youth refused survey	20	1

dren had other obligations or decided not to continue with the interview. Another 20 children refused to participate.

Additional baseline sample recruitment detail, including a sample flow chart at baseline, can be found in Appendix A. Figure 2.1 describes the *analytic* sample used in each component of the study.

Baseline Sample. The initial sample included a fairly even representation of youth by gender, included 30 percent racial/ethnic minority members. By design with our purposive sampling of service and component, approximately 57 percent of families had a parent in the Army, and nearly 20 percent in the Air Force. Approximately 37 percent of the families were in the National Guard or Reserve. The majority of families were in the mid or senior enlisted

Figure 2.1
Study Components and Sample Sizes

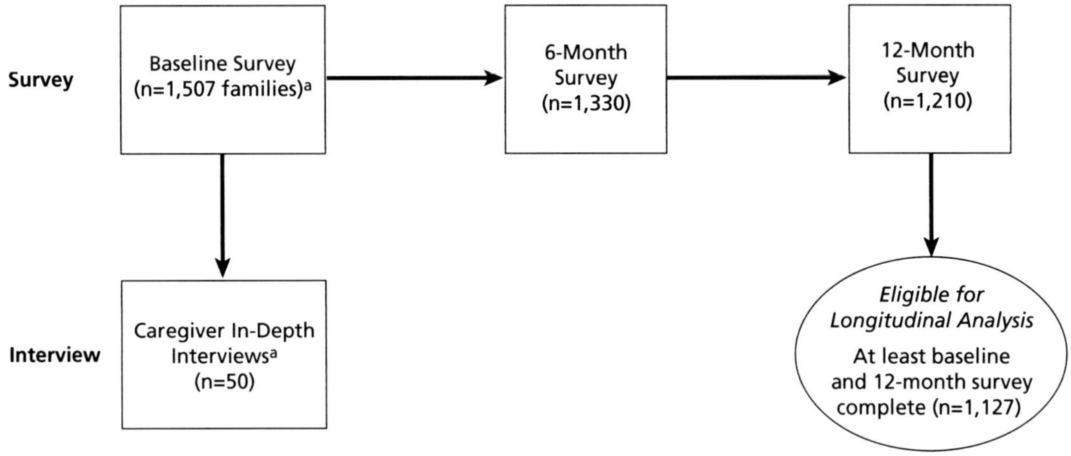

[a]The total number of qualitative caregiver interviews equals 100. An additional 50 caregivers not included in the survey component were interviewed as well. These caregivers were not eligible for the main study because their children were all under the age of 11 years, but were recruited for qualitative interviews instead.

RAND *TR913-2.1*

rank or pay grade (67 percent). Approximately 28 percent of the sample did not attend *Operation Purple®* in 2008.

Longitudinal Sample. For the analysis described in the rest of the study report, we focused on the longitudinal data analytic sample. This included all families with surveys at least from the baseline and 12-month waves (n=1,127). Table 2.3 presents the key demographic characteristics of this analytic sample at baseline, 6 months, and 12 months.

Table 2.3
Demographic Characteristics of the Longitudinal Analytic Sample at Each Survey Time Point

Demographic Characteristics	Baseline	6 Months	12 Months
Youth age (mean, SD)	12.8 (0.05)	13.2 (0.05)	13.8 (0.05)
Youth gender (% female)	48	47	48
Youth race/ethnicity (%)			
White	74.3	74.4	74.3
African American	10	10	10
Hispanic	5.0	4.9	5.0
Asian	1.3	1.3	1.3
Other	9.1	9.1	9.1
Caregiver age (mean, SD)	38.5 (0.18)	39.0 (0.18)	39.5 (0.18)
Caregiver gender (% female)	95	95	95
Caregiver relationship to youth (% biological or adoptive parent)	94.6	94.7	94.6
Caregiver education (%)			
High school or less	13.7	14.0	13.7
Some college	48.4	47.6	48.4
College or more	37.3	37.6	37.3
Caregiver employed outside home (%)	57.8	61.5	58.5
Housing (%)			
On military installation/base	21.7	19.9	18.2
Own home, off-base	67.0	68.9	69.7
Rent, off-base	11.3	11.2	11.9
Attended *Operation Purple®* in Summer 2008	72.9	72.9	72.9

NOTES: The slight difference in racial/ethnic composition at Wave 2 (6 months) is a result of the longitudinal sample eligibility criteria. To be eligible for longitudinal sample inclusion, participants had to have at least baseline and Wave 3 completed, but not necessarily Wave 2. Descriptive statistics are based on observed data and are not weighted.

Table 2.4 summarizes military and deployment history characteristics of the analytic sample.

Sample Attrition. Approximately 15 percent of families left the study entirely before the final 12-month survey. The remaining 10 percent not included in the final analytic sample

Table 2.4
Military and Deployment Characteristics of the Longitudinal Analytic Sample at Each Survey Time Point (n=1,127)

	Baseline	6 Months	12 Months
Military Characteristics			
Service			
Army	56.7	56.7	56.7
Navy	17.2	17.1	17.2
Air Force	19.8	20.1	19.8
Marines	5.3	5.1	5.3
Coast Guard[a]	0.1	0.1	0.1
Component			
Active	61.3	60.9	61.3
Reserve	38.7	39.1	38.7
Rank			
E1–E4	5.7	5.4	5.7
E5–E6	33.5	33.7	33.5
E7–E9	30.7	30.7	30.7
Officer	30.0	30.1	30.0
Number of years in military (mean, SD)	16.8 (0.2)	16.8 (0.2)	16.8 (0.2)
Deployment Characteristics			
Deployed at time of survey	38.1	25.7	14.8
Deployed at some point during study period	57.0	56.1	57.0
Return from deployment during study period (post baseline)	37.9	38.0	37.9
Total months of deployment pre-study period (2001–2008) (mean, SD)	15.1 (0.4)	15.1 (0.4)	15.1 (0.4)
Number of deployments pre-study period (2001–2008)	2.1 (0.1)	2.1 (0.1)	2.1 (0.1)
At least one deployment in Iraq or Afghanistan	65.6	65.6	65.6

[a] The Coast Guard was dropped from the final analytic models due to low sample size.

NOTES: Approximately 13% had no experience with parental deployment (10% Army, 15% Navy, 21% Air Force, 15% Marines; 12% Active duty, 16% Guard/Reserve). Descriptive statistics are based on observed data and are not weighted.

were either part of an incomplete youth–caregiver pair at baseline and thus were dropped from this analysis, or were missing a 12-month survey. We assessed how the sample of those who left the study after baseline differed from those who remained in the study. A larger percentage of the sample who left were African Americans (14 percent of the departing sample compared with 10 percent of the remaining sample, $p<.05$), from the Active component rather than Reserve component (68 percent of the departing sample compared with 61 percent of the remaining sample, $p<.05$), mid-grade enlisted (45 percent of the departing sample versus 33 percent, $p<.01$), and did not return from a deployment during the study period if deployed at baseline (79 percent versus 62 percent, $p<.01$). In addition, the sample who left the study reported more loss of contact with other military families, more deployment-related difficulties (both youth and caregiver report), and more youth emotional difficulties, as reported on the Strengths and Difficulties Questionnaire (all $p<.05$).

Baseline Findings Provided Foundation for Longitudinal Analyses

Results from our baseline survey were analyzed and published in December 2009 (Chandra et al., 2010a). Those findings provided the analytic foundation for the subsequent longitudinal work presented here. The baseline findings are briefly summarized here to set the context for the follow-on analyses presented in this report.

At baseline and after controlling for family and service member characteristics, youth in this study sample had more emotional difficulties compared with national samples. Older youth in the study sample reported significantly more school, family, and peer-related difficulties with parental deployment ($p<.01$). Length of parental deployment and poorer non-deployed caregiver emotional well-being was significantly associated with a greater number of challenges for study participants both during deployment and deployed parent reintegration ($p<.01$). Family characteristics (e.g., living in rented housing) were also linked with difficulties with deployment.

We used these baseline findings to identify the outcome domains and covariates for the remainder of the analyses described in this report. We expected that the relationships we noted at baseline would persist across the study period. We also hypothesized that youth and caregivers experiencing a return of a deployed parent during the study period would experience reductions in self-reported difficulties.

The Study Focused on Four Outcome Domains

In this section, we summarize the key outcomes of interest and the set of covariates that we included in the analytic models. These outcomes and covariates were derived from our literature review (see Chapter One) and the baseline analyses (see the previous section). We describe each measure in this section, and provide additional detail on psychometric properties in Appendix B.

Outcomes of Interest (or Dependent Variables)

The analytic models focused on four domains of interest. Findings related to youth outcomes are summarized in Chapter Three, and findings on caregiver outcomes are described in Chapter Four. All outcomes are oriented toward problems, such that higher scores translate into more self-reported difficulty.

Youth Well-Being. This domain included outcomes of caregiver and youth reports of emotional difficulty; caregiver report of youth social functioning (peer and family); and youth report of academic issues (academic engagement), anxiety symptoms; and problem behaviors. Table 2.5 summarizes the outcomes used in this model and which items were youth- or caregiver reported. Additional detail on these measures is provided in Appendix B.

- **Emotional difficulties.** The Strengths and Difficulties Questionnaire (Goodman, 2001) included 20 items on conduct and attention problems, getting along with peers and family members, and sadness or anxiety, and was completed by both youth and caregivers. This measure has population-based norms upon which to compare the study sample (SDQ, 2009). The range for this scale is 0–40, with higher values indicating more emotional difficulties.
- **Anxiety symptoms.** The Screen for Child Anxiety Related Emotional Disorders (SCARED; Birmaher et al., 1999) included five items, such as feeling frightened for no reason and difficulty sleeping. The range for this scale is 0–10, with higher scores indicating more anxiety symptoms. Youth who reported a score of 3 or more meet a symptom threshold meriting follow-up clinical assessment for an anxiety disorder.
- **Peer and family functioning.** These scales were based on the Pediatric Quality of Life Inventory (PedsQL) Parent Report for Teens (Varni et al., 2006). The 3-item peer functioning scale inquired about how often youth experience problems getting along with other kids, kids not wanting to be their friend, and getting teased by other kids. The range of this scale is 0–12, with higher scores indicating more difficulties engaging with peers. The 4-item family functioning scale included questions about how often youth experience problems participating in family activities, keeping up with responsibilities, getting along with the family, and talking about feelings or personal problems with a parent. The range of this scale is 0–16, with higher scores indicating more difficulties in family functioning.
- **Academic engagement.** This 6-item scale asked youth about being late to school, being ready for class, and other related items (Rosenthal and Feldman, 1991). The range of the scale is 0–24, with higher scores indicating more problems.

Table 2.5
Youth Well-Being Measures by Report

Measure	Youth Report	Caregiver Report
Emotional difficulties	×	×
Anxiety symptoms	×	
Peer functioning		×
Family functioning		×
Academic engagement	×	
School connectedness	×	
Problem behaviors	×	

- **School connectedness.** Many studies have shown that youth who feel "connected" to their school (e.g., "I feel close to people at this school," "I feel safe in this school," etc.) perform better academically and have fewer emotional and behavioral issues (Resnick et al., 1997; You et al., 2008). This five-item scale assessed the degree to which youth felt connected to their school. Scores can range from 0 to 20, with higher scores indicating less connectedness.
- **Problem behaviors.** The Problem Behavior Frequency Scale (PBFS) (Crick and Bigbee, 1998; Farrell et al., 2000) consists of 16 common items that all youth responded to; the original scale consists of 24 items. Using this scale, we assessed youth problem behaviors in the past six months, scored based on the number of times the behavior was reported from "never" to "20 or more times." Youth 11 to 14 were not asked about substance use or use of a weapon to hurt others. The range of the scale is 0–120, with higher scores indicating more problem behaviors.
- **Mental health service use.** We queried caregivers and youth about whether they had sought and obtained mental health services in the past six months, whether the services were for deployment-related issues, and what type of services (formal, or informal mental health care) they had used. We included these items for two reasons. First, we wanted to characterize service need and use among the *Operation Purple®* applicant pool. Second, this variable allowed us to identify any particular barriers to service use that could inform policy and program recommendations.

Youth Deployment Experience. This outcome measure includes four scales—two focused on deployment-related challenges and two focused on reintegration-related challenges (they were developed for this study; see Appendix B for more detail). Each scale was completed by the caregiver and by the youth. These questions were used only for families who had any deployment experience before and/or during the study period. The caregiver scale is made up of 10 items (range is 0–10 with a higher score indicating more difficulties). The youth scale includes 9 items (range is 0–9, with a higher score indicating more difficulties). Both scales are dichotomized (yes/no). The deployment scales include items related to missing school activities, having more responsibilities at home including caring for siblings, and feeling sad or lonely without the deployed parent.

Similar to the deployment challenges scales, new reintegration scales were created for this study, based on findings from the pilot study and expert review. The caregiver and youth scales ask questions about difficulties with reintegration (after the deployed parent returns) such as "getting to know his/her deployed parent (spouse/partner) again." Both scales were made up of six items, with each item coded as a dichotomous response (yes/no). Each scale has a range of 0–6, with higher scores indicating more difficulties.

At the six-month follow-up survey, we asked youth one open-ended question about their perceptions of whether life was different for them at school when their parent was deployed and what aspects were different. Common responses were grouped into four nonexclusive categories by members of the research team: emotional manifestations (e.g., child feels stressed) (23.5 percent); behavioral (e.g., child is more likely to get into trouble) (28.20 percent); changes in routine (40.3 percent); and other, including "just different" (20 percent).

Caregiver Well-Being. Based on the literature review, we identified several key outcomes of interest in this domain: caregiver self-reported emotional well-being, report of hassles with household stressors, relationship stressors, and parenting stressors. These measures are also described in detail in Appendix B.

- **Emotional well-being.** The 5-item Mental Health Index (MHI-5) (Berwick et al., 1991; McCabe et al., 1996) assessed the caregiver's mood in the month preceding the interview (e.g., felt calm and peaceful, felt so down in the dumps that nothing could cheer you up). Scores could range from 0 to 20, with the higher score indicating worse emotional well-being.
- **Hassles.** A shortened version of Hall, Williams, and Greenberg's (1985) daily hassles inventory assessed the degree to which caregivers were bothered by various household, relationship, and parenting responsibilities. Factor analysis was used to determine which items should be grouped differently or split into each of these three areas or subscales. The subscales are described below.
  - **Household hassles.** This included seven household hassles in the six months prior to the interview. Hassles included having too many responsibilities; taking care of family members other than the youth in the study; changing roles or responsibilities in the family or marriage; experiencing financial difficulties, such as not being able to afford things for your family or owing money; not enough time to do the things you want to do; worrying about being able to meet your obligations at work; and problems getting along with your family. Scores ranged from 7 to 28, with higher scores indicating more hassles.
  - **Relationship hassles.** Relationship-related hassles in the six months prior to the interview were also assessed. Factor analysis identified a 4-item scale: experiencing divorce, problems with growing apart/in different directions from the deployed parent, physical or verbal abuse, and general difficulties with the deployed parent. Scores ranged from 4 to 16, with higher scores indicating more hassles.
  - **Parenting hassles.** A 3-item scale assessed problems with the youth's behavior, disagreements with others over discipline of the youth, and concerns about how the youth was doing in school/daycare in the past six months. Scores were summed and ranged from 3 to 12, with higher scores indicating more hassles.

Caregiver Deployment Experiences. We used three scales to assess the caregiver's own deployment experience (see Appendix B). Initially, we constructed one scale to assess deployment-related challenges. However, based on confirmatory factor analysis, the deployment scale was split into subscales: concerns about community support and concerns about the youth during deployment. The scale on concerns about community support during deployment was made up of four items (range of 0–4, higher indicating more difficulties) related to whether people in the community understood what deployment is like or what the military lifestyle entails. The scale on concerns about the youth during deployment was made up of four items (range of 0–4, higher indicating more difficulties) related to youth school difficulties and taking on more parenting responsibilities.

A seven-item scale focused on caregiver issues during the deployed parent's reintegration. The range of the scale was 0–7, with higher scores indicating more difficulties.

Independent Variables

Based on prior baseline analyses (Chandra et al., 2010a), we identified the following demographic, military, and deployment characteristics as variables that may play a role in the outcomes under study.

Demographic and Background Characteristics. We included youth age, youth gender, caregiver emotional well-being (described above), service (Army, Navy, Air Force or Marines), and component (Active or Reserve). In addition, we included two sets of variables on communication and deployment history.

Youth–Caregiver Communication Quality. We examined youth–caregiver communication quality as a factor related to youth and caregiver well-being outcomes. Because previous research has shown that parent-youth communication may have an impact on mental health problems in youth (Marta, 1997; Loeber et al., 2001; Shuli et al., 2006), we included these scales as predictors in the models. Examples of items in the youth-reported scale include "Is your caregiver a good listener?" and "Can you have your say even if your caregiver disagrees with you?" Examples of caregiver-reported items include "you can discuss your beliefs with your child without feeling restrained or embarrassed," "you are satisfied with how you and your child talk together," "you tell each other about personal problems," and "you come to a solution when you talk about a problem." The caregiver report of difficulties communicating scale ranged from 0 to 12, and the youth report of difficulties communicating with caregiver ranged from 0 to 20. Higher scores indicated more challenges.

Deployment History. Deployment history was assessed to enable us to distinguish between the experiences of deployment before the study period and during study period deployment. We defined *deployment* as any time away from home, including the training time that leads up to deployment and including U.S.-based and non-U.S. based deployment. For purpose of analysis, we included only deployments that were greater than 30 days.

We constructed several variables to capture deployment experience, including the sequencing of deployment. This included eight patterns of deployment across three time points: deployed at baseline, not deployed at 6 months, deployed at 12 months, and so forth. However, sample sizes for each of the eight patterns were small and did not yield meaningful differences. Ultimately, the final set of variables was the following:

- Cumulative months and number of deployments from 2001 to the start of the study period (2008)
- Recent months and number of deployments in the one year prior to the study period (2007 to 2008)
- Deployment experience during the study included three variables:
  - a time-varying variable on whether the parent was deployed at the time of survey administration
  - a dichotomous variable on whether the parent was ever deployed during the study period
  - a variable on whether the parent ever returned from deployment during the study period.

Other Covariates

In addition to these independent variables, we included other variables that may be related to the outcome of interest or that prior research suggests is important to account for analytically.

Youth demographic variables included youth race and caregiver demographic factors, including caregiver age, gender, employment, and education. Housing (living on base, living off base [property owner], and living off base [renter]) was also included.

Other military characteristics included in the analyses were rank and time in the military. Ultimately, time in the military was dropped from the final analytic models. We also included the location of deployment (Iraq, Afghanistan, other) and parent role in deployment (combat versus combat support).

Analytic Approach

In this section, we provide a brief overview of the general statistical approach and then outline the key quantitative analytic steps. We also present our approach to the qualitative analysis of caregiver interview data.

Survey Data Analysis

Statistical Approach. We first conducted exploratory bivariate analysis. To adjust for sample attrition, we calculated the attrition weight and reported weighted descriptive statistics. *Attrition weight* is defined as the inverse of the probability of missing an observation. We applied logistic regression to estimate these probabilities using relevant baseline variables.

We then applied general linear mixed models (McCulloch and Searle, 2001) to estimate the relationship between the outcomes of interest and key predictors, while accounting for relevant covariates. We used PROC MIXED in the general statistical software package SAS 9 (SAS Institute Inc., 2002–2004) to fit the mixed model. Most of the estimated effects and statistical tests in this report are based on the likelihood-based inference to the mixed model.

We conducted two types of tests to examine the statistical significance of a predictor in the mixed model. First, we tested whether a single entry of the coefficient is equal to 0 by the regular *t*-test, i.e., the Wald's test statistic, with degrees of freedom (d.f.) equal to the error d.f. The second test was the type III F-test in SAS, or—more formally—the general linear hypothesis test. The F-test was used to simultaneously test multivariate relationships among several entries of the coefficients. We used the F-test to examine the overall effect of a qualitative predictor. If the F-test rejected the null hypothesis, we claim that this predictor has a significant main effect. The details of the differential effects among all *m* levels are revealed by the follow-up *t*-tests for pairwise comparisons. Appendix C presents more details of the mixed model and related statistical tests implemented in this study.

Use of Multiple Comparison Adjustments. In the previous baseline analyses (Chandra et al., 2010a), we applied the conservative Bonferroni adjustment within each outcome to avoid false significant findings. In the current analyses, the main goal was to confirm the previous findings based on longitudinal analysis. Essentially, we examined a special subset of hypotheses for each outcome. The issue of multiplicity was no longer a serious concern. For example, if our interest focused on caregiver emotional well-being (MHI-5), testing it alone or together with 10,000 other factors without adjustment did not make a difference. It is true that, without adjustments, we will make many false findings. However, the chance that the MHI-5 variable was among the false findings was still .05. Based on these considerations, $p=.05$ for previously identified risk factors was deemed adequate evidence for significance in the current study.

However, p=.05 was weak evidence for other predictors that were not previously identified but that appeared significant in the longitudinal analysis.

Multiple Imputation. We also used multiple imputation methods (Rubin, 1996) to address any issues associated with missing data. The primary source of missing data was incomplete deployment history. Depending on the outcomes, there was complete deployment history information for roughly 1,100 subjects with slight variations, and missing information on one or more variables for 300 subjects (approximately 22 percent). We imputed the missing data based on service, component, and rank. We assessed the similarities between the multiple imputation method and the original mixed model analysis by comparing the significant findings. We considered the results to be similar because these two approaches generally had significant findings in common. The differences between the two sets of analyses are mainly in the specific values of the estimates and associated standard deviations, which is a common phenomenon when an alternative technical approach is used. The results based on the multiple imputation method have slightly more significant findings, possibly due to increased sample sizes. Therefore, we conclude that the original results based on complete observations are not sensitive to the missing data. Throughout this document, we focused on the results based on complete observations rather than on the multiple imputation method. Additional details about our statistical approach and multiple imputation is provided in Appendix C.

Analysis of the Quantitative Data. As briefly described in the last section, the analyses were split into two main phases. First, we wanted to explore which factors were significantly associated with the outcomes of interest throughout the study period. Second, we were interested in whether there were any notable trends in how functioning (well-being) and experience of deployment-related challenges changed over the study period, particularly for those who had experienced a deployment at baseline or during the study period, as well as the return of a deployed parent during the study period after the baseline. We included interaction terms between time and key deployment variables to note this. We also examined interactions between other covariates and time, but found that they were not significant, so they were subsequently dropped from the analysis.

In the first set of analyses, we were primarily interested in assessing which factors were significantly associated with youth and caregiver outcomes across the period. This analysis allows for testing the main effects of those variables in explaining differences between subgroups of youth and caregivers, particularly those identified as important in the baseline analyses (Chandra et al., 2010a). In addition, for those outcomes for which we had cutoff or threshold scores, we explored what variables characterized or helped to explain why some youth continued to report moderate-to-high emotional difficulties and elevated anxiety symptoms, as well as which youth reported decreases in their symptoms across time.

In the second set of analyses, we explored whether the outcomes changed over the study period. If an outcome changed across the study period, we further examined how the covariates influenced the (nonflat) trajectories. Recall the two types of covariates in the mixed model: time-invariant and time-varying. A (significant) time-invariant covariate can shift the position of the trajectory but does not change its shape. The difference in intercepts is the main effect from the first set of analysis. Here, we focus on the effects of time-varying covariates. In the models, the time-varying covariates consist of the time indicators, i.e., two binary indicators for the second and third waves, respectively, interactions between time indicator and other covariates, and real-time measurements (e.g., on-time deployment status, caregiver emotional well-being).

Subgroup Comparison. We conducted two tests for comparisons over time. First, we used time indicators to reveal whether the trajectory of the reference group is flat (no overall significance per F-test), wavy (opposite directional changes between the adjacent time points), or monotonic (neither increase nor decrease over time).

Second, we tested other time-varying effects to identify whether the trajectories differ among subgroups. The subgroups are defined by the categorical covariates describing deployment characteristics. Each group has a distinct cumulative or recent deployment history. For example, one group consists of youth whose parents have more than one year cumulative deployment from 2001 to the start of the study and no deployment during the study period. Another group of youth consists of those whose parents had less than one year cumulative deployment prior to the study period, were deployed during the study, and had not returned from deployment by the end of the study. When two subgroups do not have significant differences, they can be aggregated to a new group. Note that after the initial analysis, the deployment experience variables primarily reflect return from deployment since the baseline survey and ongoing deployment during the study period. Other analyses assessing patterns of deployment throughout the study period (e.g., deployed at baseline, back at 6 months, back at 12 months; deployed at baseline, back at 6 months, deployed again at 12 months; and so forth) did not indicate significant differences between deployment "states" and thus are not a primary focus of the report.

In Chapters Three and Four, we plot some representative subgroups' trajectories that have significant differences among each other with respect to the key outcomes. We note that cumulative and recent deployments have different impacts on different outcomes.

Logistic Regressions for Youth in the Elevated Risk Categories. For two of the outcome variables of interest, emotional difficulties and anxiety symptoms, we employed measures that had cutoff threshold scores for establishing high or elevated risk. For these outcomes, we conducted additional logistic regression analyses to identify the odds or likelihood that youth in the "elevated" categories for emotional difficulties and anxiety symptoms, respectively, stayed in that group at 12 months or moved to the lower categories. The regression models included an indicator variable for "change to the better" or "switch to the low-symptoms category." The independent variables were baseline values of the variables used in the rest of the analyses (e.g., youth age, gender, caregiver emotional well-being, and so forth). Based on caregiver report, approximately 12 of the youth in the longitudinal sample switched from high-to-moderate emotional difficulties to the lower difficulties category, although it should be noted that those with high-to-moderate emotional difficulties were more likely to leave the study post-baseline.

Caregiver Interview Data Analysis

We used standard qualitative methods (Miles and Huberman, 1994) for analyzing interview data. Three randomly selected caregiver interviews were reviewed and coded by the two principal investigators and a research assistant on the project. Using an inductive process drawing on textual data, we coded the transcripts for "mentions" based on the responses to the four areas of inquiry. Next the coders independently reviewed the notes and created their own set of codes, then met and agreed on a final set of codes. Five primary themes emerged from the interview data to be briefly summarized later: household hassles, including parenting obligations; consequences of changes in responsibilities, such as feeling overwhelmed; coping with changes in household responsibilities; quality of communication in relationship; and changes

CHAPTER THREE

The Experience of Military Youth in the Study Sample

This chapter summarizes key findings from analyses of (1) how military youth in the study sample are functioning emotionally, socially, and academically and (2) the challenges that these study participants confront that are specifically related to parental deployment and reintegration. The chapter is divided into two sections to correspond to these two questions. Each section is further divided into subsections, with findings organized by youth outcomes (e.g., emotional difficulties, anxiety symptoms).

Each section reports on findings from the longitudinal data set described in Chapter Two and follows a similar scheme.

- First, we summarize the outcomes, primarily at baseline but with attention to any notable differences in average scores at 6 months and 12 months. These outcomes include emotional difficulties, anxiety symptoms, peer and family functioning issues, academic engagement problems, risk behaviors, and deployment and reintegration challenges. We also summarize two outcomes, school connectedness and youth mental health service use, which were only included in the 6-month and 12-month surveys. Questions about these outcomes were added to provide context to the academic and deployment outcomes, but some analyses were not applied given the lack of three time points.
- Second, we describe some of the key differences by subgroups of youth with attention to five factors: youth age, youth gender, caregiver emotional well-being, service, and component. For the youth and caregiver well-being outcomes only, we also assessed the role of caregiver-youth communication quality. These analyses are drawn from the F-test for the overall significance of the factor across the study period (see Chapter Two).
- Third, we discuss effects associated with deployment history on the outcomes of interest, by examining the relative role of deployment experience both before and during the study period.
- For two outcomes—emotional difficulties and anxiety symptoms—we had threshold scores between "high" and "low" risk. For these outcomes, we also assessed the factors associated with a greater likelihood of remaining in the risk group during the study period.

Detailed data tables with results for all covariates are found in Appendix D. In the next sections, we provide brief data summaries only.

We Examined a Broad Spectrum of Outcomes Related to Youth Well-Being

Previous studies of deployment experience suggest an association between combat-related parental deployments and a negative impact on youth well-being, particularly emotionally and academically. Here, we address a broad spectrum of outcomes to understand the deployment experience of youth across a variety of domains. In this section, we describe findings for outcomes in the following areas:

- emotional difficulties
- anxiety symptoms
- peer and family functioning
- academic issues (engagement, school connectedness)
- other risk or problem behaviors.

Emotional Difficulties

We queried youth and their caregivers about youth emotional and behavioral difficulties using the Strengths and Difficulties Questionnaire. There are population-based data and cutoff scores upon which to compare the caregiver report of youth emotional or behavioral difficulties (Goodman, 2001). Overall, 30 percent of the caregivers in the *Operation Purple®* applicant sample reported moderate-to-high levels of emotional or behavioral difficulties among their children at baseline. This percentage is higher than the percentage among the national sample of youth. For example, 34 percent of youth ages 11–14 in this study reported elevated emotional or behavioral problems, compared with 19 percent of youth this age in the general population (see Figure 3.1).

From the baseline survey, we noted that caregiver report of youth emotional difficulties changed significantly from survey wave to wave ($F(2, 1913)=39.7$, $p<.01$) (see Appendix D for

Figure 3.1
A Higher Percentage of Study Sample Reported Moderate-to-High Emotional Difficulties

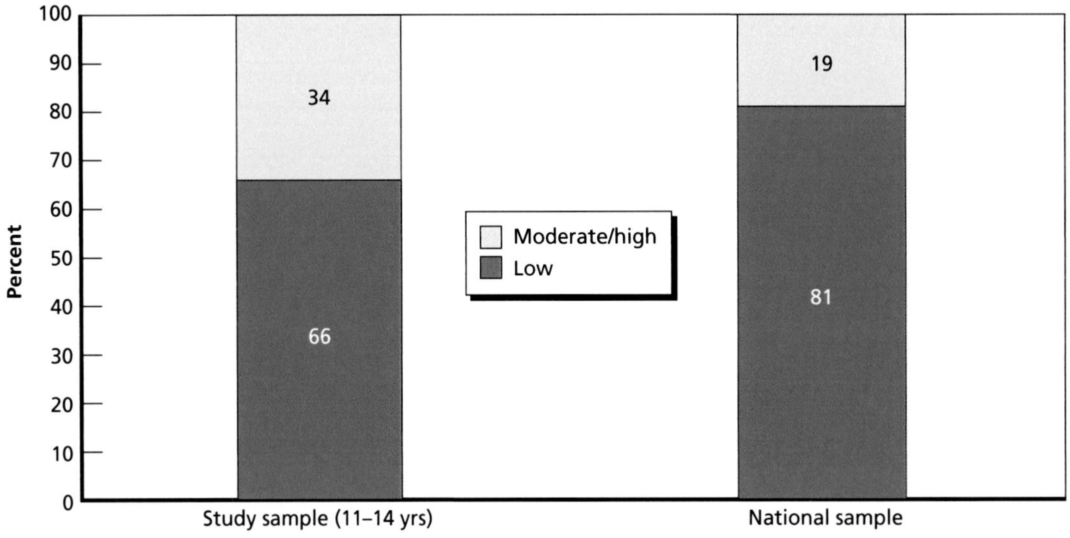

RAND *TR913-3.1*

details and Table 3.1 for mean scores by wave). This represents an average decrease between baseline and 12 months of 0.84 points (SD=0.20, $p<.01$), and an average increase between the 6-month and 12-month follow-up wave of 0.59 points (SD=.20, $p<.01$). Despite this change, the average caregiver report of emotional difficulties at each time point was still greater than the national average (Goodman, 2001). At 6 months and 12 months, nearly 30 percent of caregivers still reported difficulties in the moderate-to-high range. Given earlier discussion about the characteristics of the study sample, this finding could mean that the children in the sample are experiencing elevated emotional difficulties and hence are applying to *Operation Purple®* to address these issues. Another possibility is that caregivers in the sample may be more attuned to identifying these challenges in their children because of their age, parenting experience, or resources.

Youth participants also reported on their emotional or behavioral difficulties. Similar trends occurred for youth reports of emotional difficulties ($F(2, 1913)=40.6$, $p<.01$). Overall, the model suggests that youth in our sample reported somewhat fewer difficulties over time. The decrease was significant between baseline and 12 months (1.61 points, SD=0.22, $p<.01$) but the difference between the 6-month and 12-month survey was not significant ($p=0.1$). This translates into approximately 44 percent of participating youth reporting difficulties in the moderate-to-high range at baseline; this dropped to 38 percent at 6 and 12 months.

Differences by Group. At baseline, we noted some differences in reports of emotional or behavioral difficulties by subgroups of youth in our sample. These differences persisted with the longitudinal analyses, notably, youth gender and caregiver emotional well-being.

Youth Age. There were no significant differences in either the caregiver or youth report.

Youth Gender. Caregivers of girls reported fewer emotional difficulties than caregivers of boys ($F(1,1913)=25.4$; $p<.01$) with an average difference of 1.78 points on the 20-point scale (SD=0.35)($p<.01$). However, there was no gender difference for the *youth* report of difficulties.

Caregiver Emotional Well-Being. Caregivers in the study with poorer emotional well-being reported more youth emotional challenges ($F(1,1913)=190.0$, $p<.01$). Study youth whose caregivers reported poorer emotional well-being also reported more personal emotional difficulties ($F(1,1913)=17.4$, $p<.01$). The effects here are 0.38 and 0.12, respectively; therefore, while

Table 3.1
Mean Scores by Wave of Each Youth Well-Being Outcome Variable

Youth Outcome Variables	Baseline	6 Months	12 Months
Emotional difficulties (youth-reported)	11.5 (0.2)	10.0 (0.2)	9.7 (0.2)
Emotional difficulties (caregiver-reported)	9.9 (0.2)	8.1 (0.2)	8.5 (0.2)
Anxiety symptoms	1.9 (0.0)	1.6 (0.0)	1.6 (0.1)
Peer functioning	1.8 (0.1)	1.6 (0.1)	1.3 (0.1)
Family functioning	4.3 (0.1)	3.8 (0.1)	3.8 (0.1)
Academic engagement	4.8 (0.1)	4.3 (0.1)	4.4 (0.1)
School connectedness	NA	5.0 (0.1)	5.0 (0.1)
Risk behaviors	5.4 (0.2)	5.3 (0.2)	5.4 (0.2)

NOTES: Estimates are based on weighted data. NA = not applicable because item was not included at baseline. Standard deviations are in parentheses.

statistically significant, an increase of one point on the caregiver emotional well-being scale is associated with less than a one-point change in the youth emotional difficulties scale (suggesting an average difference of one emotional difficulty or higher rating for a difficulty on the 40-point scale). It should be noted that these analyses merely show relationships between the variables of caregiver and youth emotional well-being and do not denote directionality or causality.

Youth–Caregiver Communication Quality. Youth in the study who reported that they have difficulty communicating with their caregiver reported more personal emotional difficulties ($F(1,1913)=102$, $p<.01$). Youth-caregiver communication quality is a key factor discussed in the rest of this chapter and in Chapter Four.

Service. There were no differences observed by service.

Component. There were no differences observed by component (Active versus Reserve).

Deployment History. One of the main study questions addressed whether recent experience with deployment had a relationship with emotional difficulties during the study period compared with experience during prior deployment.

For emotional difficulties as reported by both caregiver and by youth in the study, there were no significant differences with respect to deployment experience during the pre–study period and the study period. As noted in Figure 3.2, there were no significant differences between the group that did not experience a deployment during the study period (but did experience deployments before) and the groups that had at least one month of parental deployment during the study period.

Figure 3.2
Caregiver Report of Youth Emotional Difficulties During the Study

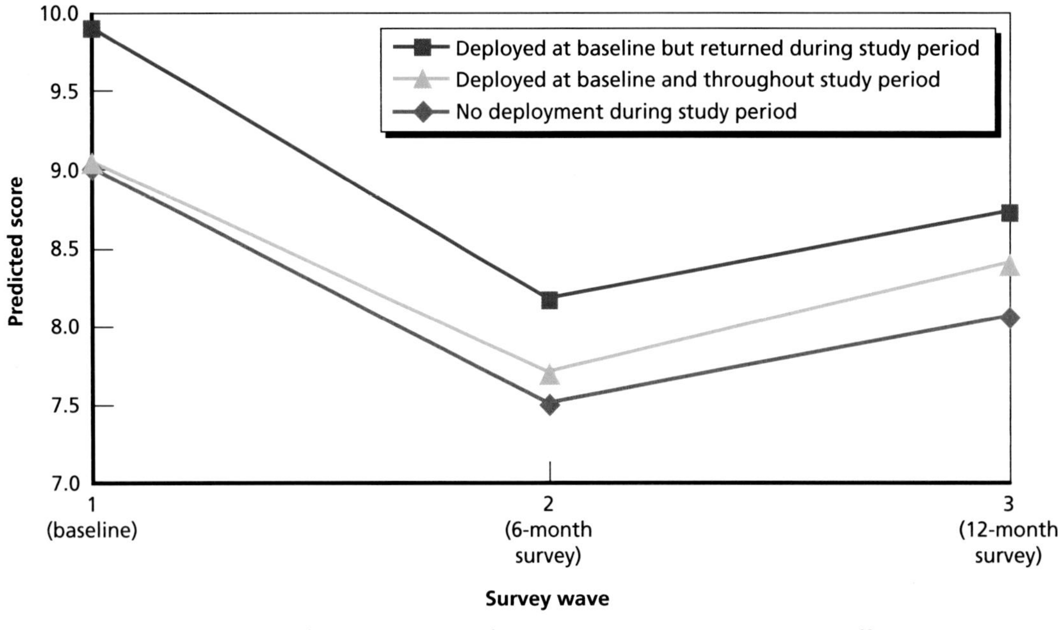

NOTE: Average predicted score for three groups defined by deployment characteristics. Differences between groups are not significant. The range of possible scores on this outcome is provided in Appendix B—Measures.
RAND *TR913-3.2*

Pre–Study Period. There were no significant differences for the cumulative history of deployment (2001 to the start of study period), or deployments that occurred in the most recent period (one year before the study period).

Study Period. There were also no significant differences in the report of emotional difficulties, whether or not the youth experienced a deployment or parental return during the study period.

Moderate-to-High Emotional Difficulties Group. Given the availability of threshold scores for emotional difficulties (moderate/high versus low), we examined whether youth in the study stayed in their baseline categories for this outcome across the study period or whether they switched categories (that is, reported more or fewer difficulties at subsequent time points). We examined which groups were more likely to report an increase or decrease in emotional difficulties (based on caregiver report) from baseline to the 12-month survey, as well as groups that were more likely to switch categories from moderate-to-high levels of emotional difficulties to low difficulties at the 12-month survey.

First, if the study family experienced the return of a deployed parent between baseline and 12 months, the caregiver was more likely to report at least some decrease in youth difficulties (OR=1.34 (95% CI: 1.1–1.9), $p<.05$). If caregivers reported increasing difficulties in their emotional well-being, they were *less* likely to report improvements in youth emotional difficulties (OR=0.94 (95% CI: 0.89–0.97), $p<.01$).

Actual switching from moderate-to-high levels of emotional difficulties at baseline to the low difficulties category at 12 months (based on caregiver report) was *less* likely among those in the study with more cumulative months of deployment prior to the study period (OR=0.97 (95% CI: 0.94–0.99), $p<.05$).

For youth report of emotional difficulties, study youth whose caregivers reported difficulties in emotional well-being at baseline were *less* likely to report improvements in emotional difficulties over the study period (OR=0.95 (95% CI: 0.94–0.99), $p<.05$). Older teens, youth having parents in the Air Force, or those with parents in higher ranks (compared with E1–E4) in our sample were less likely to improve over the study period, or less likely to move from moderate-to-high emotional difficulties to low difficulties (all $p<.01$). Other factors, such as deployed parent return and cumulative months of deployment, were not associated with youth-reported decreases in emotional difficulties.

Anxiety Symptoms

Overview. We queried youth in the sample about anxiety symptoms in the past six months using the SCARED measure. At baseline, approximately one-third of the sample reported elevated anxiety symptoms (or a cutoff score of 3 or more), requiring follow-up clinical assessment for actual anxiety disorder (see Figure 3.3). Youth who score below this cutoff score do not require a clinical assessment. It should be noted that in our longitudinal analyses, youth in the sample who reported anxiety symptoms at higher levels at baseline were more likely to leave the study after baseline.

Overall, anxiety symptoms decreased from wave to wave ($F(2, 1907)=9.2$, $p<.01$). There was a significant decrease between baseline and 6 months of 0.28 points ($p<.01$), but then no change between 6 and 12 months ($p=0.83$). As with the emotional difficulties outcome, this sample of *Operation Purple*® applicants may have been experiencing higher levels of anxiety symptoms at the time of camp application (and hence the baseline survey captured that), but overall, between baseline and 12 months, these symptoms decreased. However, it should be

Figure 3.3
A Higher Percentage of Study Sample Reported Elevated Anxiety Symptoms

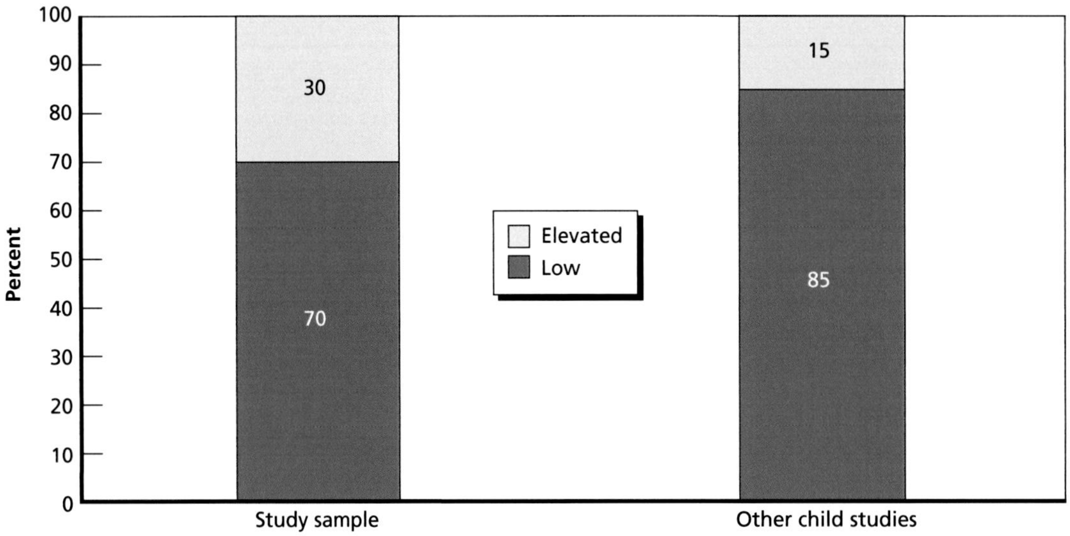

NOTE: Scores in elevated range merit a follow-up clinical assessment for anxiety disorder.
RAND *TR913-3.3*

noted that those youth experiencing higher anxiety symptoms were more likely to leave the study after baseline. Thus, we do not know if that subgroup would have continued to report elevated anxiety symptoms.

Differences by Group. At baseline, we noted some differences in anxiety symptoms by subgroups of youth in the sample. These differences persisted in the longitudinal analyses, where we also observed differences by youth age and gender as well as caregiver emotional well-being.

Youth Age. Younger teens in the study reported more anxiety symptoms than older teens (F(1,1907)=9.7, p<.01). With each year in age, there was a reduction by 0.10 points (SD=0.03) in the SCARED scale.

Youth Gender. Girls in the sample reported more anxiety symptoms (F(1,1907)=47.9, p<.01) than boys in the sample. On average, girls in the study had a score 0.64 points higher (SD=0.22, p<.01) than boys on the SCARED scale.

Caregiver Emotional Well-Being. Poor caregiver emotional well-being was associated with youth reporting greater anxiety symptoms (F(1,1907)=4.0, p<.05).

Youth-Caregiver Communication Quality. Youth in the study who reported problems communicating with their caregiver reported more anxiety symptoms than those with fewer problems (F(1,1907)=4.4, p<.05).

Service. There were no significant differences by service.

Component. There were no significant differences by component.

Deployment History. For anxiety symptoms among study participants, there were no significant differences associated with deployment experience in the pre–study period and during the study period. As noted in Figure 3.4, there were no significant differences between the group that did not experience a deployment during the study period (but did experience deployments before) and the groups that had some deployment during the study period.

Figure 3.4
Youth Report of Anxiety Symptoms—Comparison of Deployment History During Study

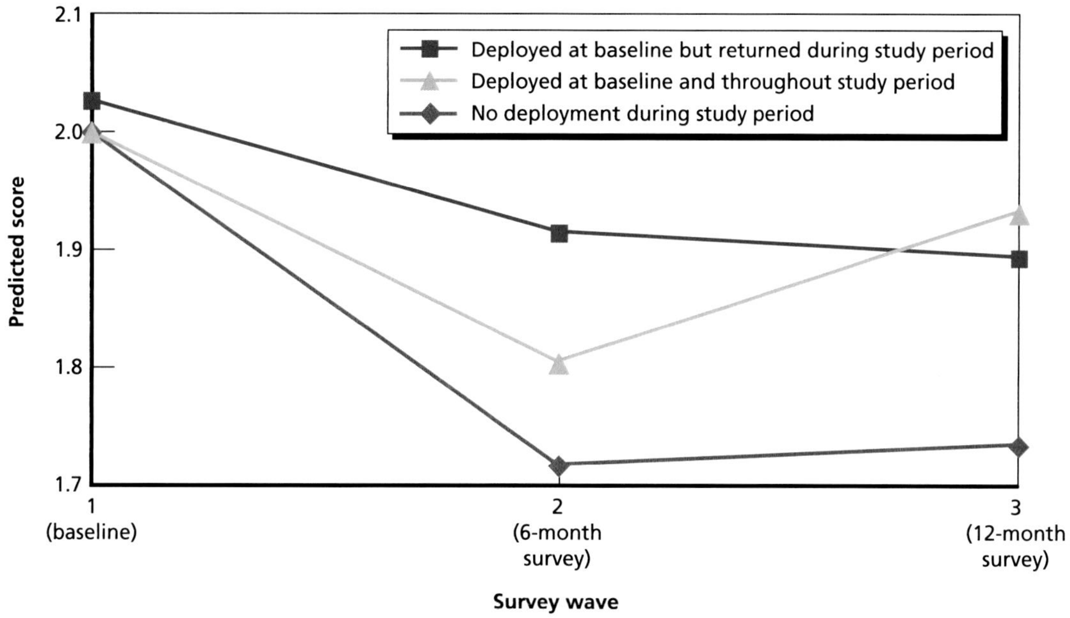

NOTE: Average predicted score for three groups defined by deployment characteristics. The difference between groups is not statistically significant. The range of possible scores on this outcome is provided in Appendix B—Measures.
RAND *TR913-3.4*

Pre–Study Period. There were no significant differences for the cumulative history of deployment (2001 was the start of the study period), or deployments that occurred in the most recent period (one year before the study period).

Study Period. While there was some difference between the group that experienced a parental return from deployment and the one that did not, the difference is not statistically significant.

Elevated Anxiety Symptoms Group. As with emotional difficulties (for which we had threshold scores), we were able to examine the factors that were most associated with youth in the sample who remained in the elevated anxiety symptoms category (cutoff score of 3 or more on the 10-point scale, suggesting the need for a follow-up clinical assessment) across the study period. We found that those youth in the study whose caregiver reported problems with emotional well-being at baseline were *less* likely to move to the low (or non-elevated) anxiety symptoms category (OR=0.92 (95% CI: 0.85–0.99), p<.05). Youth in the study with Navy parents were less likely to report a reduction in symptoms over the study period compared with Army youth (OR=0.33 (95% CI: 0.14–0.79), p<.01), but there were no other differences by branch of service.

Peer and Family Functioning Problems

Overview. We queried caregivers in the study about their child's difficulties getting along with peers (peer functioning) and their ability to engage with family members (family functioning). The items for each are scale are based on the PedsQL Parent Report for Teens (Varni, Burwinkle, and Seid, 2006) (see Appendix B). At baseline, we noted that peer functioning issues as reported by youth in our study were comparable to those found in other U.S. studies of youth (average score of 1.5 on a scale of 0–12, SD=2.2), but that family functioning problems among study participants were slightly worse than in other U.S. studies of youth (average score of 4 on a scale of 0–16, SD=3.0) (Jaycox et al., 2009).

Peer functioning issues among study participants decreased across time points, adjusting for all other covariates (F(2,1879)=18.7, p<.01). On average, peer functioning problems decreased by 0.16 points (SD=0.1) between baseline and 12 months, but this was not significant (p=0.09); the decrease of 0.19 points (SD=0.1) between 6 months and 12 months *was* significant (p<.05). Family functioning issues reported by study participants remained unchanged. The observation that family functioning issues remained comparatively higher may signify ongoing family issues in the families that applied to *Operation Purple®*, even among those who actually attended. These issues are likely not readily addressed by a one-week summer camp.

Differences by Group. Within our study sample, we noted differences by age, emotional well-being, and component.

Youth Age. Caregivers of older teens in the study consistently reported more peer functioning issues (F(1,1879)=15.6, p<.01). There were no differences by youth age for family functioning problems.

Youth Gender. There were no gender differences in peer functioning among study participants, but there were differences for family functioning (F(1,1895)=8.0, p<.01). Caregivers of boys in the study reported more family difficulties for their child compared with caregivers reporting on girls in the study (average 0.43-point difference on the scale).

Caregiver Emotional Well-Being. Among study participants, poor caregiver emotional well-being was significantly related to youth peer functioning (F(1,1879)=62.7, p<.01) and family functioning (F(1,1895)=179.1, p<.01) issues.

Youth-Caregiver Communication. Caregivers of youth in the study who reported more challenges communicating with their caregiver reported more peer functioning (F(1,1879)=4.9, p<.05) and family functioning challenges (F(1,1895)=18.1, p<.01).

Service. There were no differences by service.

Component. There were no differences by component.

Deployment History. For peer and family functioning problems among the study sample, there were no significant differences with respect to pre–study period and during study period deployment experience.

Pre–Study Period. There were no significant differences for the cumulative history of deployment (2001 was the start of study period), or deployments that occurred in the most recent period (one year before the study period).

Study Period. There were also no significant differences during the study period, whether or not the youth in the study experienced a deployment or parental return during the study period.

Academic Engagement Issues

Overview. We queried youth in the study about their ability to attend to tasks at school during the past six months, using a 6-item, 24-point scale of academic engagement difficulties (Rosenthal and Feldman, 1991). Overall, reports of academic issues among youth in the study were comparable to those in other studies of U.S. youth (average score on a 24-point scale at baseline of 4.6, SD=0.10). Over the study period, youth academic issues changed significantly for the study sample (F(2,1841)=5.8, p<.01). On average, the score on the scale decreased, but not significantly, between baseline and 12 months (p=.85), but the 6-month survey wave is significantly lower than the 12-month survey by 0.36 points (SD=0.14, p<.01). It is unclear why a pattern of decrease then increase occurred, although it may be related to the stress of the academic year, spring testing, or end-of-year fatigue. The available literature to date does not provide insight.

Differences by Group. Differences by youth age, gender, and poor caregiver emotional well-being observed at baseline (older youth, boys, and caregivers with more emotional issues reported more academic difficulties) persisted across the study period.

Youth Age. Older teens in the sample reported more academic issues compared with younger youth (F(1,1841)=19.1, p<.01)

Youth Gender. Boys in the study reported more difficulties than girls (F(1,1841)=26.5, p<.01). On average, girls had a score 0.83 points (SD=0.16) less than boys.

Caregiver Emotional Well-Being. In addition, poor caregiver emotional well-being was associated with more youth academic problems among our sample (F(1,1841)=11.3, p<.01).

Youth-Caregiver Communication Quality. Youth in the study who reported more difficulties communicating with their caregiver also reported more academic engagement difficulties (F(1,1841)=88.9, p<.01).

Service. There were no significant differences.

Component. There were no significant differences. It should be noted that among our sample, higher parental military rank was associated with fewer reported academic issues (F(1,1841)=3.9, p<.01), on average a 0.8-point (SD=0.4, p<.05) difference on the scale between junior enlisted and senior enlisted (see Appendix C for more detail).

Deployment History. For academic issues, there were no significant differences among our sample with respect to cumulative history of deployment, but there was one notable difference in the one year prior to the study period.

Pre–Study Period. In our sample, if a youth had had a parental deployment in the year prior to the study period, he or she reported more academic engagement issues (F(1,1841)=6.4, p<.01) during the study. This translates to a 0.9-point difference on average (SD=0.3, p<.01) on the 24-point scale.

Study Period. There were no significant differences during the study period, whether or not the participating youth experienced a deployment or parental return during the study period.

Problem Behaviors

Overview. Youth in the study were asked about their engagement in problem or risk behaviors, such as getting into fights with peers, getting into trouble at school, and using alcohol or other substances over the past 30 days (one month). We used the Problem Behavior Frequency Scale (Farrell et al., 2000). Overall, youth reported problem behaviors at rates comparable to those in other U.S. studies (Crick and Bigbee, 1998; Farrell et al., 2000). For the purpose of this analysis, we only compared groups of youth on items that all youth answered, regardless of age. The scale ranged from 0 to 60 points (average at baseline 5.3 (SD=.01)), with higher values indicating more problems.

Across time, there was no difference in youth reports of problem behaviors (F(2,1913)=0.4, p=0.70). In other words, the trend was flat.

Differences by Group. Differences found at baseline by youth age and gender persisted, with older teens and boys in the study reporting more problem or risk behaviors. These gender and age differences are consistent with other studies of U.S. youth (Crick and Bigbee, 1998; Farrell et al., 2000).

Youth Age. Older teens in the study reported more problems than younger teens ($F(1,1913)=4.5$, $p<.05$).

Youth Gender. In addition, boys in the study reported more problem than girls ($F(1,1913)=21.8$, $p<.01$); on average, girls reported problem behavior scores 1.8 points ($SD=0.4$) *lower* than boys on a 60-point scale.

Caregiver Emotional Well-Being. There were no differences in youth-reported risk behaviors.

Youth-Caregiver Communication Quality. Youth in our study who reported more communication problems with their caregiver also reported greater engagement in risk behaviors ($F(1, 1913)=64.4$, $p<.01$).

Service. There were no significant differences.

Component. There were no significant differences.

Deployment History. For risk behaviors, there were no significant differences with respect to deployment history.

Pre–Study Period. There were no significant differences for the cumulative history of deployment (2001 was the start of the study period) or prior-year deployment.

Study Period. There were no significant differences during the study period, whether or not the youth in our study experienced a deployment or parental return during the study period.

Youth Deployment Experience

This section summarizes youth experiences with parental deployment and parental return (reintegration). These analyses are restricted to those youth in the study sample who had experienced at least one parental deployment before and/or during the study period. We primarily describe factors contributing to youth deployment experiences, including the reasons youth experienced deployment and reintegration difficulty and which subgroups fared better or worse with deployment. We rely on the established scales of deployment and reintegration difficulties (Chandra et al., 2010; also Appendix B). In addition, we summarize mental health service use by youth that is specifically related to deployment. The key variables examined for subgroup differences in the prior section are assessed here, except for youth-caregiver communication. Given that there was no association in bivariate analyses with deployment outcomes, we dropped this variable in these analytic models.

Challenges for Youth During Deployment

Overview. As described in Chapter Two and Appendix B, the research team created two scales for deployment challenges, one each for the caregiver and youth reports. Figure 3.5 summarizes youth-reported challenges during deployment.

During deployment, youth in the study reported that *dealing with life without the deployed parent* (68 percent) and *helping caregiver deal with life without deployed parent* (68 percent) were most difficult. Another frequently endorsed concern was *not having people in the community understand what deployment is like* (45 percent).

Figure 3.5
Youth-Reported Challenges During Parental Deployment

NOTE: Percentages are not mutually exclusive.
RAND *TR913-3.5*

We also queried caregivers about youth difficulties during deployment using a scale we created specifically for this study (see Appendix B). Caregivers in the study endorsed these items as the most difficult challenges for their child during deployment: *Dealing with life without the deployed parent* (72 percent) and *feeling overwhelmed by new responsibilities at home* (57 percent).

Differences by Group. We noted key differences in youth deployment experience by youth age, caregiver emotional well-being, cumulative deployment experience, and component.

Youth Age. Caregivers of older teens in the study reported more deployment challenges (F(1,1255)=9.9, p<.01), as did older teens themselves (F(1, 1414)=9.4, p<.01).

Youth Gender. Girls in the study reported more difficulties during deployment than boys (F(1,1414)=17.8. p<.01), but there were no differences by caregiver report.

Caregiver Emotional Well-Being. Caregivers in the study with emotional well-being issues also reported more deployment challenges for their children (F(1,1255)=33.7, p<.01).

Service. There were significant differences by service only for youth report of deployment difficulties (F(1, 1414)=4.1, p<.01). The difference was primarily between Marines and Army youth in the study.

Component. There were significant differences by component for caregiver report only. Reserve component caregivers in the study reported 0.45 more youth difficulties (F(1, 1414)=14.4, p<.01) during deployment than Active caregivers in the study.

Deployment History. For deployment history, there were significant differences based on prior experience of parental deployment.

Pre-Study Period. Families in the study that had experienced more total months of deployment from 2001 to the start of the study period also reported more deployment-related challenges (caregiver report: F(1,1255)=3.3, p<.05) (see Figure 3.6). In fact, compared with study youth who had experienced one year or less of total deployment, caregivers of youth in the study who experienced 13 or more months since 2001 reported 0.27 more deployment-related challenges (SD=0.24). If a youth in the study experienced a parental return in the year prior to the study period, the youth reported fewer deployment challenges during the study period ($F(1, 1414)=4.1$, $p<.05$).

Study Period. Deployment at the time of a survey wave was associated with more caregiver-reported deployment challenges ($F(1,1255)=5.6$, $p<.05$). However, as shown in Figure 3.6, those youth in the study who had more cumulative months of parental deployment before the study period still reported more difficulties than those who had lower pre–study period deployment regardless of study period deployment experience. This finding may reflect the general experience that more parental deployment months can continue to affect or influence youth difficulties regardless of immediate or proximal deployment experience. Another explanation for this finding could be linked to retrospective consideration or recall bias. In this, youth may recall difficulties with parental deployment that may not be as readily apparent within a current deployment experience.

Deployment Experience: Gaining Some Qualitative Context. To provide additional context for the challenges youth and caregivers face associated with deployment experiences, we examined responses administered at the six-month follow-up survey to an open-ended question as to whether, in the youth's perception, life was different for them at school when their parent was deployed and, if it was different, what aspects were distinct. Given that only 22 percent of the sample reported that life was different for them at school, we report only frequencies of responses among those individuals and did not analyze further.

Figure 3.6
Comparison of Youth Deployment Difficulties: Pre–Study Period Deployment Versus Study Period Deployment

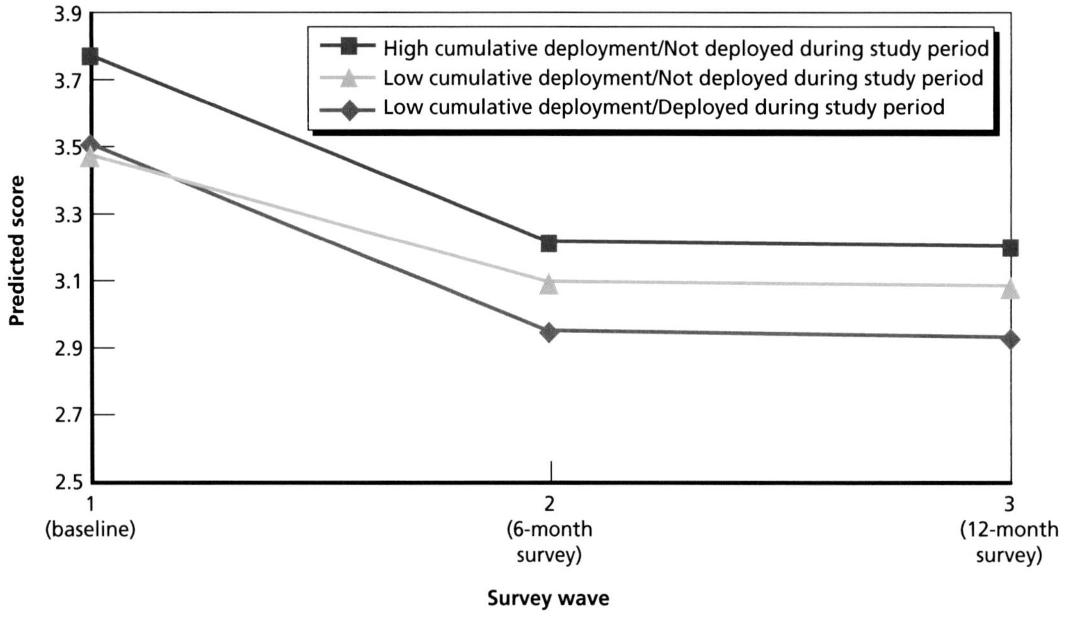

NOTES: Average predicted score for three groups was defined by deployment characteristics. Difference between high cumulative deployment pre-study was significantly different from either low cumulative deployment group. Low deployment is 12 months or less, not including zero. High deployment is 13 months or more. The range of possible scores on this outcome is provided in Appendix B—Measures.

RAND *TR913-3.6*

Fifty-one percent of youth in the study reported experiencing emotional or behavioral difficulties when their parent was deployed. Of these, 38 percent cited difficulties concentrating on schoolwork, 15 percent felt sad or lonely, and 15 percent felt more anxious. Seventeen percent reported having issues with schoolwork while their parent was away. Of the study youth citing these issues, 66 percent expressed concerns about getting help with homework. Seventeen percent of the sample reported home/family environment changes, for example, difficulties with juggling household maintenance tasks, and 11 percent reported that friends treat them differently when their parent is deployed.

Challenges for Youth During Reintegration

Overview. We also queried caregivers and youth about reintegration challenges using items we created (see Chapter Two for more detail) (Figure 3.7). Youth in the study endorsed *fitting returning parent back into home routine* (54 percent) and *worrying about the next deployment* (47 percent) most frequently.

Overall, caregivers in the study endorsed *fitting the deployed parent back into the home routine* (62 percent) and *getting to know deployed parent again* (52 percent) as the most difficult challenges for their child during reintegration.

Differences by Group. We observed differences in youth reintegration experience by youth age, gender, and cumulative deployment experience.

Youth Age. Older teens in the study reported more reintegration-related difficulties $(F(1, 1453)=9.4, p<.01)$.

Youth Gender. Girls in the study also reported more reintegration challenges $(F(1,1453)=23.2, p<.01)$.

Caregiver Emotional Well-Being. Caregivers in the study who reported emotional difficulties themselves also reported more challenges for their child during reintegration $(F(1,1187)=55.1, p<.01)$.

Service. There were no differences by service.

Figure 3.7
Youth-Reported Challenges During Parental Reintegration

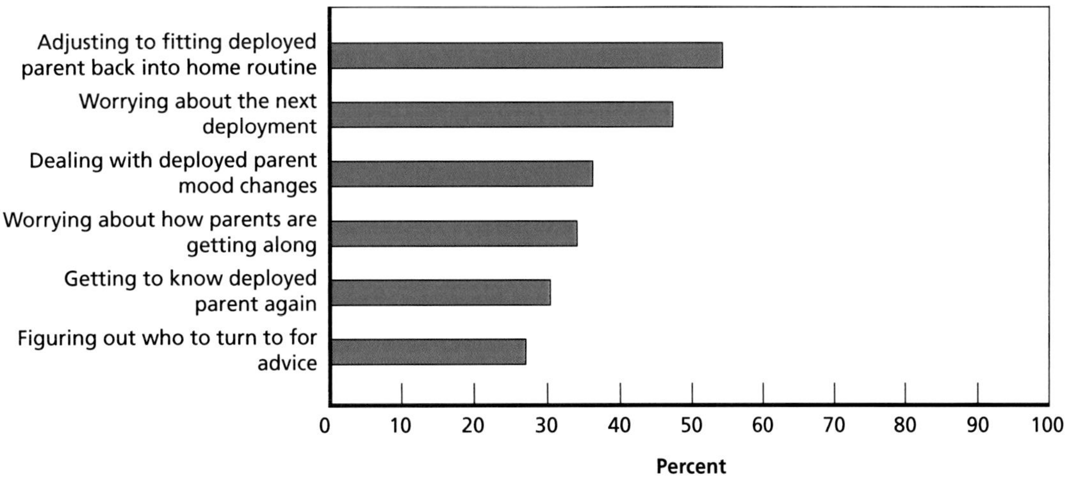

NOTE: Percentages are not mutually exclusive.
RAND *TR913-3.7*

Component. Reserve component caregivers in the study reported more reintegration challenges for their children than Active caregivers ($F(1, 1187)=4.3$, $p<.05$).

Deployment History. For deployment history, there were significant differences based on prior experience of parental deployment (see Figure 3.8).

Pre-Study Period. Prior deployment history, or cumulative months of deployment from 2001 to the study period, were related to more reintegration challenges as identified by both caregivers and youth in the study (caregiver: $F(1,1187)=7.9$, $p<.01$); youth: $F(1,1453)=6.4$, $p<.01$).

Study Period. There were no significant differences in reintegration issues. Reintegration issues did not significantly increase or decrease, even among those youth in the study experiencing a parental return during the study period.

Other Outcomes

In addition to the outcomes assessed in the previous sections, we also explored two outcomes related to school connectedness and youth mental health service use. These questions were implemented at the 6-month and 12-month survey only; thus, the usual analyses do not apply.

Figure 3.8
Comparison of Youth Reintegration Difficulties: Pre-Study Period Deployment Versus Study Period Deployment Experience

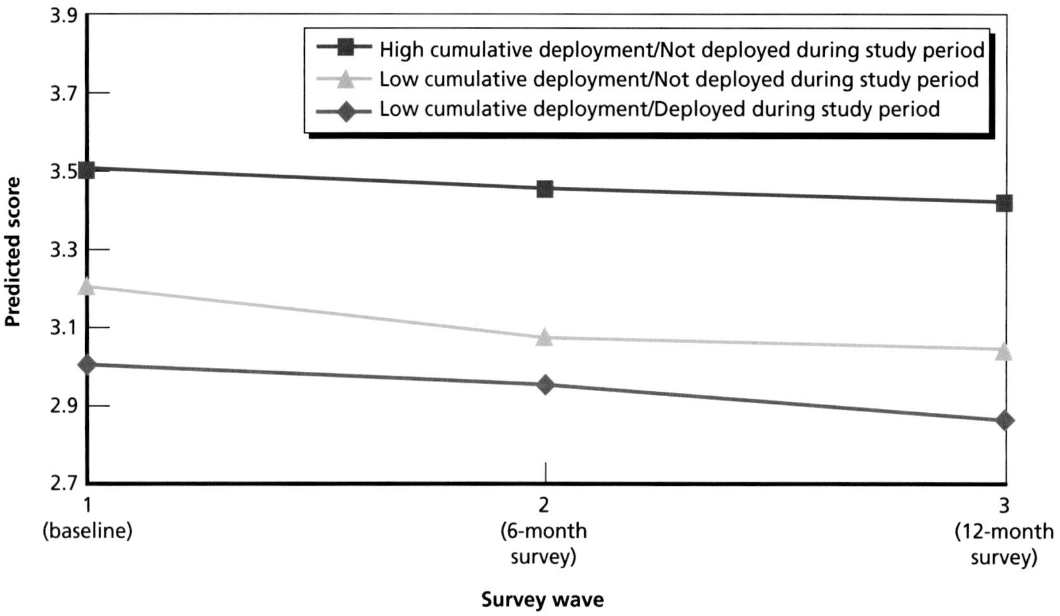

NOTES: Average predicted score for three groups was defined by deployment characteristics. These groups were selected to show difference between deployment exposure and deployment history. Difference between high cumulative deployment and each low cumulative deployment group is statistically significant. Low deployment is 12 months or less, not including zero. High deployment is 13 months or more. The range of possible scores on this outcome is provided in Appendix B—Measures.

RAND *TR913-3.8*

School Connectedness

Overview. Studies of military youth have suggested that frequent moves and transition issues may explain some difficulties in academic functioning (Engel, Gallagher, and Lyle, 2006; Chandra et al., 2010b). To place these academic engagement issues in context, we also explored how youth felt about their schools using the School Connectedness Scale (Resnick et al., 1997). These questions were asked on follow-up surveys only, and thus we do not have a baseline survey or analyses across the study period. Therefore, the analysis focused on factors of youth well-being and component but also included school location and residential moves.

Overall, we found that the average school connectedness score among our study youth was comparable to averages found in other studies of youth (Resnick et al., 1997; You et al., 2008). Since many studies do not report the scale but rather individual items, we compared these items to a study of civilian youth by You et al. (2008). Based on a Welch t-test, we found that the following items had significant differences:

I feel close to people at school. The military youth in the study sample reported less connection than in the civilian study ($p<.05$).

I am happy to be at this school. The military youth in the study sample reported less connection ($p<.01$).

Teachers treat students fairly at this school. The military youth in this sample felt more connected on this item or more positive about teachers ($p<.01$).

I feel safe at this school. The military youth in this sample felt more connected/more positive on this item ($p<.01$).

I feel part of this school. There were no differences between the two samples.

Differences by Group. *Youth Well-Being.* We assessed whether those who were less school-connected had more emotional or behavioral difficulties, consistent with other studies. We found no differences in emotional difficulties scores, but those with higher scores for anxiety symptoms were less connected to their school ($\beta=1.9$, $p<.01$). As expected, academic engagement issues and school connectedness were highly associated ($\beta=0.2$, $p<.01$).

Youth-Caregiver Communication. Youth in the study who reported more problems communicating with caregivers also reported more problems feeling connected to school ($\beta=0.20$, $p<.01$).

Change in Schools During Study Period. Approximately 25 percent of the sample had changed schools in the past year, a figure that may include the change from middle school to high school. There was no difference in their school connectedness scores. There was no association between either deployment status at the time of the survey or deployment history and school connectedness.

School Location. We examined whether location of the school was a factor and did not find any significant difference by whether youth attended school on-base or off-base. Those youth who aspired to complete college (approximately 82 percent of the sample) reported more school connection than those who did not ($\beta=-0.68$, $p<.05$). There was no difference in reports of school connectedness for those who aspired for military careers (approximately 32 percent of the overall sample) versus those who did not.

Component. We noted that Active component families in the study reported less school connection than Reserve component families ($\beta=-0.68$, $p<.05$). There were no differences by service or rank.

Youth Mental Health Needs and Deployment

Overview. In addition to examining youth well-being and deployment-related challenges experience, we asked caregivers in the study (at the 6-month and 12-month surveys) about youth mental health needs and whether those needs were addressed by a mental health specialist (e.g., licensed psychologist) and/or other supports, such as a chaplain, family member, or friend. We also queried caregivers about whether the need was related to deployment. These analyses were not longitudinal, so changes during study period are not presented. Approximately one-fifth of the caregivers reported that their child needed mental health services, and two-thirds of those caregivers attributed this need to deployment.

Differences by Group. There were no major differences in reported mental health need by most characteristics.

Youth Age. No differences.

Youth Gender. No differences.

Service. Army and Navy caregivers in the study reported more need than the other services, but only at six months ($p<.05$).

Component. No differences.

High-Risk Groups (High/moderate emotional difficulties, elevated anxiety symptoms). We also examined whether at-risk groups, such as those who scored within the moderate-to-high range for emotional difficulties and anxiety symptoms described previously, were perceived by their caregivers as needing mental health services. Of those who needed mental health services in our sample, one-third had moderate-to-high emotional difficulties and one-fifth had elevated anxiety symptom scores.

Service Utilization. The vast majority of youth in our study (89 percent) who needed mental health support received services. For those in our sample who received services, most received these services from a mental health provider/specialist (84 percent at 6 months; 87 percent at 12 months). Another 35 percent (at 6 months) and 52 percent (at 12 months) went to a chaplain, family friend, or friend. Some of these visits were in addition to specialist visits.

Barriers to Service Use. Reported (or perceived) barriers to treatment varied slightly among study participants over the two time periods (6- and 12-month interview). At six months, the top two reported reasons that youth in the study did not receive mental health support were access (14 of the 22 endorsed this barrier) and a long wait to be seen (6 of 22 caregivers gave this reason). At twelve months, lack of access explained why 15 of the 23 youth did not receive mental health services. Perceptions that services or treatment would not benefit their child explained why 10 of 23 youth in the study did not receive services at 12 months.

Summary

In summary (see Table 3.2), the longitudinal data analyses identify factors associated with emotional, social, and academic difficulties among our study participants. Older teens in our sample reported more academic difficulties, while younger teens reported more anxiety symptoms. Girls in the study also reported more anxiety symptoms. Among our participants, caregiver emotional well-being was positively associated with youth emotional well-being. In addition, youth–caregiver communication problems were associated with youth functioning difficulties.

Table 3.2
Summary of Key Predictors of Well-Being Difficulties Across Three Waves

Factor	Emotional Difficulties	Anxiety Symptoms	Social Problems	Academic Engagement Problems	Problem/Risk Behaviors
Youth age		× (younger)	× (older)	× (older)	× (older)
Youth gender	× (girls)	× (girls)		× (boys)	× (boys)
Poor caregiver emotional well-being	×	×	×	×	
Poor youth–caregiver communication quality (youth reported)	×	×	×	×	×
Service/component					
Pre–study deployment (yes/no)				×	
During study deployment (yes/no)					

We also found that caregiver-reported youth deployment difficulties decreased from survey wave to wave on average (see Table 3.2). However, if a deployment was being experienced during the study period, the reported challenges remained higher than if a deployment only preceded the study period. Youth-reported difficulties (deployment and reintegration) remained fairly stable over the study period, with no significant increases or decreases.

Within our sample, older teens, youth experiencing more months of parental deployment, and those with poorer caregiver emotional well-being reported more difficulties (Table 3.3). Girls reported more reintegration issues overall. In addition, Reserve component caregivers reported more youth deployment and reintegration challenges.

Table 3.3
Summary of Key Predictors of Youth Deployment and Reintegration Difficulties Across Three Study Waves

Factor	Youth-Reported Deployment Problems	Caregiver-Reported Deployment Problems	Youth-Reported Reintegration Problems	Caregiver-Reported Reintegration Problems
Youth age	× (older)	× (older)	× (older)	
Youth gender	× (girls)		× (girls)	
Poor caregiver emotional well-being		×		×
Service	×			
Component		×		×
Pre–study deployment (more months of deployment)		×	×	×
Study period deployment history		×		

CHAPTER FOUR

The Experience of Caregivers in the Study Sample

This chapter focuses on the experiences of caregivers in this *Operation Purple®* applicant study sample. The first section summarizes key findings regarding caregiver emotional well-being as well as challenges caregivers confront in managing the household and maintaining their relationship with the deployed parent. The second section describes difficulties specifically related to spousal deployment and reintegration.

As in Chapter Three, each section is organized by outcome, with attention to general findings, differences by subgroups of caregivers, and comparison of the effects associated with deployment history. Detailed tables are found in Appendix E.

On Average, Self-Reported Caregiver Well-Being Improved During the Study Period

This section presents results in the following areas:

- caregiver emotional well-being
- household hassles
- relationship hassles
- parenting hassles.

As discussed in Chapter One, prior studies of deployment experience suggest an association between combat-related deployments and a negative impact on spouses' well-being. In this study, we further explore this relationship and also examine hassles related to caregiver management of the household, the relationship with the deployed parent, and parenting. These areas may considerably change or shift for the caregiver during a deployment. We found that, overall, in our sample, caregivers' emotional well-being improved on average from wave to wave in the yearlong study period, though there were important variations among subgroups, as we describe below.

Caregiver Emotional Well-Being

Overview. We assessed the emotional well-being of caregivers using the 5-item Mental Health Index (MHI-5). Scores range from 0 to 20, with higher scores indicating greater problems. The mean MHI-5 for caregivers in our sample at baseline was 5.3 (SD=0.10). Over the study period, there was a decline on average in caregiver reported emotional health difficulties ($F(2, 1944)=4.2$, $p<.05$) (see Table 4.1). Improvement between baseline and 6 months was not

Table 4.1
Mean Scores by Wave of Each Caregiver Well-Being Outcome Variable

Caregiver Outcome Variables	Baseline	6 Months	12 Months
Emotional well-being (MHI-5)	5.4 (0.1)	4.9 (0.1)	4.9 (0.1)
Household hassles	13.9 (0.1)	13.0 (0.1)	12.7 (0.1)
Relationship hassles	5.6 (0.1)	5.4 (0.1)	5.7 (0.1)
Parenting hassles	5.8 (0.1)	5.5 (0.1)	5.3 (0.1)

NOTES: Estimates are based on weighted data. Standard deviations are in parentheses.

significant, but change between baseline and 12 months was marginally significant (p=.07). Estimates are based on weighted data.

Differences by Group. The results from the longitudinal analysis indicate that there were differences in caregiver emotional well-being by service, component, and quality of caregiver-youth communication.

Youth Age. There were no significant differences.

Youth Gender. There were no significant differences.

Caregiver-Youth Communication. Caregivers in the study who reported difficulties communicating with their child also reported problems with their emotional well-being (F(1, 1944)=94.9, p<.001)

Service. While we noted differences at baseline between Navy caregivers in our study and those in other services, those differences were not significant in the longitudinal analyses (F(3,1944)=2.21, p=0.08).

Component. Caregivers in the study affiliated with the National Guard and Reserve (or Reserve component) reported significantly worse emotional well-being compared with those in the study affiliated with the Active component (F(1,1944)=21.5, p<.001).

Deployment History. For deployment history, there were significant differences based on whether the family experienced parental return from deployment during the study period (see Figure 4.1).

Pre–Study Period. Prior deployment history, or cumulative months of deployment from 2001 to the study period, were not significantly related to caregiver emotional well-being at the final assessment or baseline (p=0.9).

Study Period. Within our sample, if a caregiver experienced deployment at the time of interview, his or her emotional well-being was worse compared with caregivers not experiencing a deployment (F(1, 1944)=11.6, p<.001). In addition, if a deployed parent returned home during the study period, the caregiver reported better emotional health (F(1, 1944)=14.9, p<.001) than in prior reports during the deployment. As shown in Figure 4.1, there was a remarkable difference in the trajectories of caregivers whose spouse/partner was continuously deployed during the study period (difficulties increased) and caregivers whose partner returned midyear (difficulties decreased).

Household Hassles

Overview. A deployment may translate into loss of emotional and instrumental support for caregivers, which, in turn, may lead to increased household obligations. To determine group differences in household challenges experienced during a deployment, we queried caregivers in

Figure 4.1
Caregiver Emotional Well-Being (Using the MHI-5): Comparison Between Continuous Study Period Deployment and Deployed Parent Return

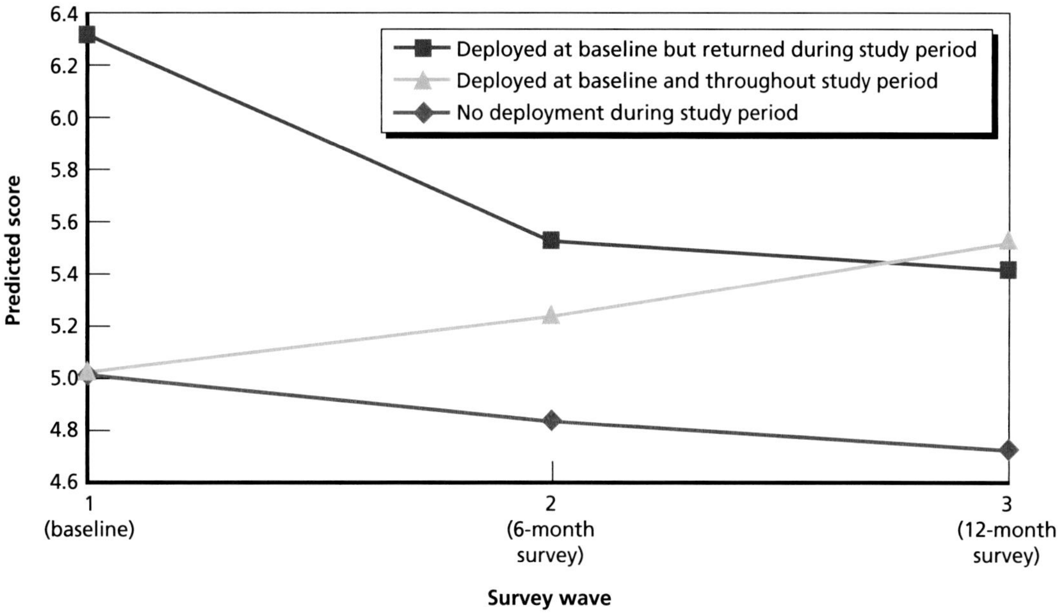

NOTES: Average predicted score for three groups was defined by deployment characteristics. Difference between deployed during study period and returned during study period is statistically significant. The range of possible scores on this outcome is provided in Appendix B—Measures.
RAND *TR913-4.1*

the study sample about the degree to which household-related challenges bothered them. We used the Hall et al. (1985) scale of daily hassles (Appendix B). At baseline, the average score among our sample was 13.8 (SD=0.14) on this scale, which ranged from 7 to 28. The average report of household hassles decreased over the course of the study (F(2,1930)=14.9, p<.001). A possible interpretation of this finding is that caregivers who applied to *Operation Purple*® for their child/children may have been experiencing greater difficulties managing the household at the time of application and thus wanted "respite" from those household duties (e.g., childcare) for the week of the camp. The reduction across the study period may reflect a return to average levels on this measure. Since those with greater stress were more likely to leave the study post-baseline, however, some caregivers with the greatest household stress level are missing in the longitudinal sample, possibly masking the true level.

Differences by Group. There were differences in self-reported household hassles by caregiver emotional well-being, caregiver-youth communication quality, and component.

Youth Age. No significant differences.

Youth Gender. No significant differences.

Caregiver Emotional Well-Being. Caregiver emotional well-being was significantly associated with variation in household hassles, with those experiencing poorer emotional well-being also reporting more hassles (F(1, 1930)=474.5, p<.001).

Caregiver-Youth Communication Quality. Caregivers were asked about the quality of their communication with the study youth. Caregivers who reported poorer communication with the study youth also reported more household hassles (F(1,1930)=18.9, p<.001).

Service. No significant differences.

Component. Caregivers in the study sample from the National Guard and Reserves (Reserve component) reported significantly more household challenges compared with those in the study sample affiliated with the Active component ($F(1,1930)=22.5$, $p<.001$); a 1.6 point difference (SD=0.2) on the 28-point scale.

Deployment History. For deployment history, there were no significant differences based on pre–study period history or experience during the study period.

Pre–Study Period. No significant differences.

Study Period. No significant differences.

Relationship Hassles

Overview. The research suggests that deployment can have a negative impact on the relationship between the caregiver and the deployed service member (Schumm et al., 2000; Karney and Crown, 2007). We also used the Hall et al. (1985) daily hassles scale to assess relationship difficulties. The average relationship hassles scale for caregivers in our study was 5.8 (SD=0.07) at baseline, which ranged from 0 to 16 (or 4 to 16 for the study sample). This average score increased slightly over the study period or average score wave to wave ($F(2, 1931)=7.1$, $p<.01$).

At baseline, *changing roles in the marriage* (30 percent) and *problems growing apart from the partner* (25 percent) were the most frequently endorsed relationship hassles among caregivers in our study sample.

Differences by Group. Relationship hassles varied by the emotional well-being of the caregiver and by component.

Youth Age. No significant differences.

Youth Gender. No significant differences.

Youth Emotional Well-Being. Caregivers experiencing poorer emotional well-being also reported more relationship hassles ($F(1, 1931)=348.3$, $p<.001$).

Caregiver-Youth Communication. There was no relationship of communication quality with relationship difficulties.

Service. There were no significant differences.

Component. Reserve component caregivers in our study reported more challenges in their relationship with the service member than those caregivers in our study from the Active Component ($F(1, 1931)=9.7$, $p<.001$).

Deployment History. For deployment history, there were no significant differences based on pre–study period history, but there were differences based on whether a deployment was experienced during the study period.

Pre–Study Period. No significant differences.

Study Period. If caregivers experienced a deployment at the time of the interview, they reported *fewer* relationship hassles than if the partner was at home ($F(1, 1931)=10.7$, $p<.001$).

Parenting Challenges

Overview. Using the Hall et al. (1985) daily hassles scale, we queried caregivers in the study sample about a range of challenges they might have experienced in the six months prior to the interview. This included challenges related to parenting the focal youth. Of these, concerns about *youth's behavior in school* (42 percent) and *problems with youth's behavior* (31 percent) most bothered caregivers. The average report of parenting hassles among our sample decreased over the course of the study ($F(2,1941)=14.7$, $p<.001$). As described in the section on household hassles, this average decline may have occurred because caregivers were at a heightened period of stress at the time of *Operation Purple*® application.

At baseline, caregivers in the study reported being most bothered by *not having time to do things they wanted to do* (53 percent) *and having too many responsibilities at home* (47 percent).

Differences by Group. Self-reported parenting hassles were related to the gender of the youth, the emotional well-being of the caregiver, and communication quality.

Youth Age. No significant difference.

Youth Gender. Caregivers of boys in the study reported more parenting challenges than caregivers of girls (F(1, 1941)=42.8, p<.001). This is about a 0.73-point difference (SD=0.11) on the 12-point scale.

Youth Emotional Well-Being. Caregivers in the study who were experiencing poorer emotional well-being also reported more parenting problems (F(1, 1941)=140.5, p<.001).

Caregiver-Youth Communication. Caregivers in the study who reported better communication with the study youth also reported fewer parenting challenges (F(1, 1941)=132.9, p<.001).

Service. No significant differences.

Component. No significant differences.

Deployment History. For deployment history, there were no significant differences based on pre–study period history, but there were differences based on whether a deployment was experienced during the study period.

Pre–Study Period. No significant differences.

Study Period. If caregivers experienced a deployment during the study period, they reported *fewer* parenting hassles than if there was no study period deployment (F(1, 1941)=6.7, p<.01).

Spousal Deployment Can Present Significant Challenges for Caregivers

In this section, we summarize the challenges that caregivers confront that are specifically related to the deployment and reintegration of a spouse or partner.

Caregiver Experiences During Deployment

We created deployment and reintegration challenges scales specifically for caregiver personal experiences (see Appendix B).

Figure 4.2 summarizes caregiver challenges during deployment. Key challenges in our study sample were *taking on more responsibilities at home caring for youth* (83 percent) and *helping youth deal with life without the deployed parent* (80 percent).

Differences by Group. We found differences in deployment difficulties by the gender of the caregiver's youth and the emotional well-being of the caregiver.

Youth Age. No significant differences.

Youth Gender. Caregivers of boys in the study reported more youth difficulties during deployment than caregivers of girls (F(1, 1408)=10.7, p<.001).

Caregiver Emotional Well-Being. Caregivers in the study who had poorer emotional well-being reported more youth deployment-related difficulties (F(1, 1408)=57.4, p<.001) and more limited community support during deployment (F(1, 1155)=103.4, p<.001).

Service. No significant differences.

Figure 4.2
Caregiver Challenges During Deployment

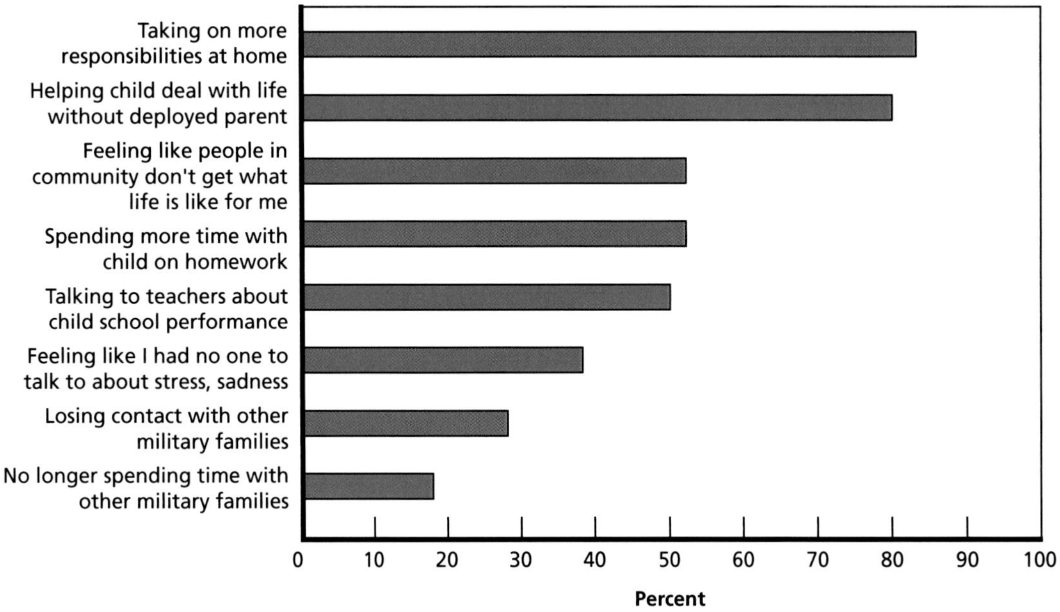

NOTE: Percentages are not mutually exclusive.
RAND *TR913-4.2*

Component. Reserve component caregivers in the study reported more deployment difficulties related to a lack of community support ($F(1, 1155)=27.9$, $p<.001$).

Deployment History. The impact of deployment history varied according to whether the deployment occurred prior to the study or during the study period.

Pre–Study Period. Those caregivers in the study whose spouses had 13 or more months of deployment reported more difficulties with a lack of community understanding or support than those caregivers in the study who had experienced fewer cumulative months ($F(2, 1155)=8.2$, $p<.001$).

Study Period. No significant differences.

Results from In-Depth Interviews with Caregivers About Deployment-Related Experiences

To provide further context for understanding caregiver mental health issues and sources of stress, we supplemented the caregiver surveys with a qualitative substudy involving 50 caregivers. The purpose was to learn about the ways in which a service member's deployment may affect a caregiver's daily obligations and relationship with the deployed service member and communication with him or her, and to provide insight about how caregivers cope with these changes. Qualitative interviews were conducted with caregivers (only female, given comparatively the small number of male caregivers in the study sample) who had experienced at least one previous deployment. Findings are briefly presented here. For more in-depth analyses, see unpublished RAND reseach by Lara-Cinisomo et al., entitled "A mixed-method approach to understanding the experiences of nondeployed military caregivers."

The interviews were guided by six areas of inquiry: (1) deployment experience; (2) the caregiver's relationship to the youth and deployed parent; (3) changing caregiver roles during and after deployment; (4) mood; (5) sense of self (e.g., help with homework, household management); and (6) the quality of caregiver's communication with the deployed parent during deployment.

Changes During Deployments. The qualitative interviews highlighted the type of changes in household and parenting obligations that caregivers experienced during deployment. For example, the caregivers we interviewed emphasized the need to take on household tasks and parenting obligations that were normally handled by the deployed service member. Household tasks included taking on new roles, such as managing the family's finances. Increased parenting obligations included added carpool trips and helping youth with homework on topics less familiar to the caregiver.

Consequences of Changes. Although many caregivers we interviewed reported their willingness to take on added obligations, these did take a toll. For instance, caregivers described the emotional impact of the added stress as well as the benefits, such as learning new skills (finances) and becoming more independent. For some, however, the impact meant having to make a professional sacrifice, such as reducing hours at work and negotiating work schedules with employers.

Coping. As a result of the household and parenting changes, the caregivers we interviewed reported using a wide range of strategies to cope with those changes, including reaching out to family and friends and paying for services they could not take on (e.g., lawn care, household repairs). The caregivers also talked about enduring the changes in obligations and finding ways to deal with it all.

Caregiver Experiences During Reintegration

Figure 4.3 summarizes caregiver reported challenges during reintegration. Key caregiver challenges during reintegration were *fitting deployed parent back into the home routine* (71 percent) and *rebalancing youth responsibilities* (61 percent).

Figure 4.3
Caregiver Challenges During Reintegration

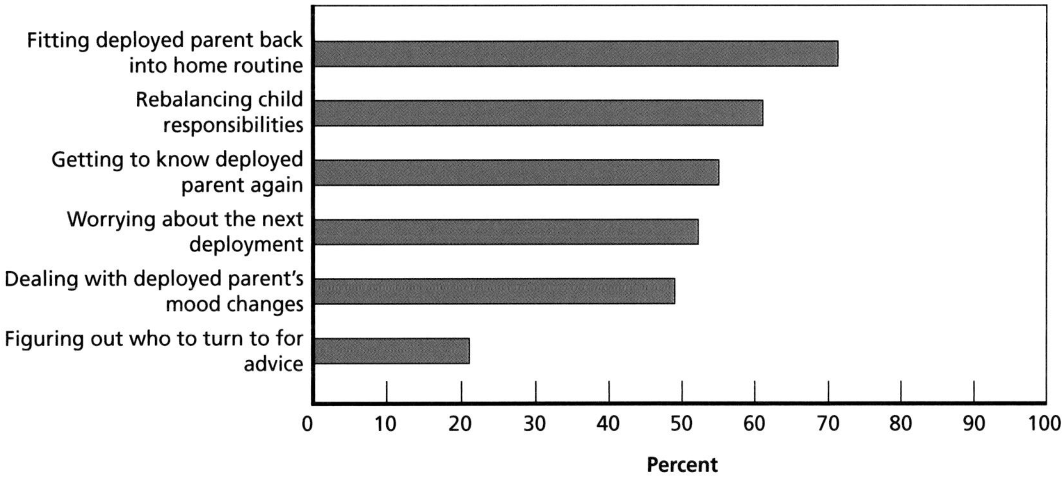

NOTE: Percentages are not mutually exclusive.
RAND *TR913-4.3*

Differences by Group. We noted differences in reintegration by caregiver emotional well-being and component.

Youth Age. No significant differences.

Youth Gender. No significant differences.

Caregiver Emotional Well-Being. Caregivers who had poorer emotional well-being reported more reintegration related difficulties ($F(1, 1249)=128.4$, $p<.001$).

Service. No significant differences.

Component. Reserve component caregivers in the study reported more reintegration challenges than Active component caregivers ($F(1, 1249)=9.4$, $p<.001$).

Deployment History. For deployment history, there were differences based on pre–study period history.

Pre–Study Period. Those caregivers in the study with 13 or more deployment months reported more difficulties during reintegration than those who had experienced fewer cumulative months ($F(2, 1249)=10.1$, $p<.001$).

Study Period. No significant differences.

Summary

In summary, we found that the emotional well-being of caregivers in our study sample varied by component of their service member, with Reserve component caregivers in the study sample reporting poorer emotional well-being. In addition, we found differences in the experiences of daily hassles or stressors. In our study sample, reported household challenges varied by component and quality of family communication. Relationship issues were greatest for Reserve component caregivers in the study sample and for those not experiencing a current deployment.

Parenting issues were greater for caregivers of boys. Finally, caregiver emotional well-being was the most salient variable across all three types of challenges, with poorer emotional well-being associated with more challenges (see Table 4.2). Caregivers who applied for *Operation Purple®* for their children may be experiencing greater difficulties and more household, parenting, and relationship stressors; hence, they seek the respite of camp. However, these caregivers tend to be older and to have more years of parenting experience. Thus, they may be able to better articulate how they feel about the stress in their lives as represented on the hassles scales.

We also found that deployment and reintegration challenges for caregivers in the study were related to their emotional well-being (Table 4.3). Concerns about lack of community support during deployment and reintegration challenges were greater among those in the study from the Reserve component and those experiencing more months of deployment.

Table 4.2
Summary of Predictors Associated with Caregiver Well-Being and Hassles Across Three Study Waves

Factor	Emotional Well-Being Difficulties	Household Problems	Relationship Problems	Parenting Problems
Youth age				
Youth gender				× (boys)
Poor caregiver emotional well-being	—	×	×	×
Poor youth–caregiver communication quality (caregiver reported)	×	×		×
Service				
Component	×	×	×	
Pre–study deployment (yes/no)				
During study deployment (yes/no)	×		×	×

Table 4.3
Summary of Predictors Associated with Caregiver Deployment and Reintegration Difficulties Across Three Study Waves

Factor	Concerns About Youth During Deployment	Lack of Community Support During Deployment	Reintegration Challenges
Youth age			
Youth gender	× (boys)		
Poor caregiver emotional well-being	×	×	×
Service			
Component		×	×
Pre–study deployment (more months of deployment)		×	×
Study period deployment			

CHAPTER FIVE

Conclusions and Recommendations

This chapter summarizes study findings, presents our conclusions, and offers several recommendations. The first section includes a summary of the major study findings, with attention to what the findings may mean in the context of the sample characteristics and in comparison with the initial baseline survey analyses. The subsequent sections outline the recommendations for policy and programs related to supporting military families as well as future research. Program recommendations provided directly by the study participants are summarized in Appendix F.

Study Findings and Conclusions

This study had two main hypotheses. First, we expected that factors that were associated with greater numbers of reported difficulties during the baseline survey would persist across the three survey waves. The study's main conclusion was that four factors were strongly associated with greater youth or caregiver deployment-related difficulties across the three survey waves: caregiver emotional well-being, cumulative months of parental deployment, component (for caregiver outcomes), and reported difficulties in youth–caregiver communication quality. The associations between caregiver emotional well-being and cumulative months of deployment and youth difficulties found in these analyses are consistent with the baseline findings. However, the follow-up analyses also revealed new findings related to component and youth–caregiver communication quality that augment the baseline findings.

The second hypothesis was that youth and caregivers experiencing the return of a deployed parent during the study period (post-baseline) would experience reductions in difficulties when compared with families that did not experience a parent return. This hypothesis was upheld for caregivers with respect to reported emotional difficulties, but not for the other outcomes under study. Caregivers who experienced the return of the deployed parent after baseline reported a greater reduction in difficulties compared with those caregivers whose partner/spouse did not return during the study period.

Throughout the report, we have referenced the unique characteristics of the sample, as military families who were seeking a program. Therefore, it is important to contextualize the findings appropriately. We note that study families may have been experiencing more difficulties at the time of their *Operation Purple*® application than other military families more broadly. At the same time, the families applying to *Operation Purple*® may have access to resources that other families do not have and may be better attuned to family difficulties. Thus, the absolute level of problems reported among our study sample may be an over- or under-estimate of problems among all military youth. Regardless, determining which subgroups of participating families who experienced relatively more or fewer difficulties informs how to better target program content for those seeking services.

Caregiver Emotional Well-Being Was Highly Associated with Youth Well-Being and Deployment-Related Challenges

Poor caregiver emotional well-being was associated with greater reported youth emotional, social, and academic difficulties. Further, if caregiver emotional health difficulties persisted or increased over the study period, youth difficulties did not diminish during the study. Among our study participants, caregiver emotional well-being was also related to greater stressors for the caregiver, including challenges maintaining the household, parenting, and relating to the deployed parent. Given the nature of these analyses, we are unable to discern the directionality of the relationship between caregiver emotional well-being and youth difficulties. It could be that youth challenges create difficulties for the parent, resulting in his or her comparatively worse emotional health. Similarly, youth may be affected by the well-being of their parent, thus affecting their health. The reciprocal influence of these factors on one another is supported in the civilian literature (Caplan et al., 1989; Chang, Halpern, and Kaufman, 2007). The findings presented in this study point to the importance of examining the interrelationships between caregiver and youth emotional and social well-being, and both may serve as targets for intervention.

Cumulative Months of Deployment Were Also a Significant Factor

Those families in our study that experienced a greater number of total months of parental deployment (13 months or more) also reported more youth emotional difficulties. In addition, these difficulties did not diminish over the study period. Families in the study with more months of deployment reported more problems during both deployment and reintegration. Further, although experiencing a deployment during the study period was a factor driving differences in caregiver emotional well-being, the number of deployment months prior to the study period was more significant than the number of deployment months during the study period. We also noted that cumulative months of deployment were related to both caregiver-reported and youth-reported youth difficulties with reintegration. There could be a few reasons for this finding. It may be easier to bring to the surface difficulties related to parental deployment in hindsight (or retrospectively) rather than at the time the deployment is occurring, or it could be a function of recall bias. Another explanation is that the measure may be detecting a longer-term influence of the strain of more months of parental deployment, regardless of when these months are experienced (lagging effects). Given that we only observed a relationship between cumulative deployment history and reported deployment difficulties based on caregiver report, it could reflect a cognitive ability of caregivers to link youth difficulties with prior history.

Participating Caregivers with Spouses in the Guard and Reserve Reported More Challenges Than Their Counterparts in the Active Component

Guard and Reserve caregivers in the study sample reported more difficulties with emotional well-being, in addition to more overall challenges during and after the deployment period. For instance, these caregivers reported more hassles during the transition period between deployment and reintegration and less community understanding of their deployment experience. As described earlier, it may be difficult for Guard and Reserve families to gain access to services (Castaneda et al., 2008). Guard and Reserve caregivers in our study sample may represent a unique subgroup of this population who have greater difficulties such that they are actively seeking support for the hassles they experienced. On the other hand, they may represent a more "networked" subgroup of Guard and Reserve families, who have more resources than other Reserve component families.

The Quality of Communication Between Caregivers and Youth Was Highly Associated with Family Functioning

Among our study sample, the quality of family communication was related to how well families were functioning. Those families in our study reporting poorer youth–caregiver communication also reported more problems with youth well-being. As described earlier, poor family communication may be a reason why the sample applied to *Operation Purple®*. For example, if caregivers found it difficult to communicate with children about deployment, they may have also thought that military peer networks would be a helpful outlet for their children. Thus, we do not know whether the communication quality is worse in the sample relative to other military families. While our analyses used this factor to explain differences in youth and caregiver emotional well-being, it could also be treated as an outcome for intervention in subsequent research.

Major Challenges During Deployment Included Difficulties Maintaining the Household

Given the need to understand the most salient challenges for families during the phases of deployment, we also summarize study findings regarding priority concerns *during deployment* for both caregiver and youth in the study. Across the study period, we noted that both caregivers and youth in the study cited difficulties with taking on more household responsibilities. For caregivers, this included more responsibilities in parenting, and for youth it included taking care of siblings. In addition, both caregivers and youth in the study sample reported difficulties confronting life without the deployed parent, and caregivers noted that they had to find ways to help their children make that transition and become accustomed to the absence of their parent. Youth and caregivers in the study also reported difficulties during deployment stemming from what they perceived as a lack of community understanding of what life was like for them during this period. This was particularly an issue for caregivers from the Reserve component.

Adjusting to the Deployed Parent's Return Brought Some Challenges

Caregivers and youth in the study noted that reintegration of the deployed parent, while a welcome experience, also brought challenges of readjusting to the deployed parent's presence and fitting that parent into the home routine. Caregivers in the study described difficulties in rebalancing childcare responsibilities while still ensuring that the deployed parent had the necessary time to adjust to home life. Notably, however, caregiver emotional well-being did improve upon the return of a deployed partner, particularly when compared with caregivers in the study whose partners were continuously deployed during the study period.

Youth in this study, on the other hand, did not experience this type of improvement if their parent returned, although it is possible that such improvement may occur but take longer to observe. Youth in the study also reported that understanding their deployed parent again, particularly if that parent experienced mood changes, was difficult.

Improvements in Some Outcomes May Be Related to Deployment Timing, Sample Composition, Survey Timing, and Regression to the Mean

While this study had the benefit of three time points, three time points may still not allow for full analysis of how deployment experience changes and whether and how youth and caregiver effects diminish or increase across time points. Coupled with our inability to anchor all families before the deployment (exposure), we are unable to discern if the slight decrease we observed during the study period on some of the outcomes continues to decrease or increases again. These effects could be more cyclical.

For example, we examined other factors that may contribute to the decrease in emotional and social difficulties and found that factors related to higher SDQ scores at baseline, such as caregiver emotional well-being, did not fully explain the reduction. Further, we assessed such factors as *Operation Purple*® attendance and whether there was a deployment or return from deployment during the study period. None of these factors was significantly associated with the changes observed. It should be noted that most of our significant decreases, on average, were between the first and second waves, but that the decrease leveled off after that.

A possible explanation is that the baseline survey occurred at a time of heightened anxiety among families, hence their application to *Operation Purple*®. Thus, after the camp, caregivers saw improvements in their child, or they simply felt more rested and able to handle the stress at home. However, our assessment did not identify a significant difference in emotional outcomes for those who attended camp versus those who did not. Further, we note that those families in our study that reported more youth emotional difficulties were more likely to leave the study after baseline. Thus, the longitudinal sample has some attrition bias, and we may not be capturing the change across time for those youth with greater challenges.

An additional reason for the reported improvement on average could be a result of regression to the mean, or the phenomenon that a variable that might be higher on its first measurement may be closer to the center of the sample distribution on a later measurement. Regardless, some factor that we did not measure may explain this slight improvement from wave to wave.

Recommendations

Based on our research, we offer suggestions for policy and program development, as well as future research. First, we summarize key policy recommendations.

Policy and Program Implications

The study offers suggestions for policy and program development that may address the challenges that youth and caregivers confront during and after deployment. These recommendations are particularly salient for those families who are seeking programs or other types of supports for their children, as was true of the *Operation Purple*® applicants. These suggestions correspond to the key factors identified in the analysis. These recommendations are primarily intended for military organizations that fund military family support programs, including the Department of Defense. However, the civilian, nongovernmental sector should also be involved in considering these recommendations.

- **Review the availability of support programs and services, including mental health services for caregivers.**

Among our study participants, caregiver emotional well-being was an important factor associated with both caregiver and youth well-being. Thus, ensuring the availability of and access to mental health services for spouses and youth who may benefit from those services is an important step. However, as noted earlier, we do not know the directionality of the association between caregiver and youth emotional well-being (it could be bidirectional); therefore, considering the emotional wellness components of programs targeting both populations may be needed.

The study findings, both quantitative and qualitative, also indicate that the caregivers in our study sample are under stress from new household responsibilities and youth caretaking challenges as well as changes in their relationship with the deployed parent. Based on our caregiver semistructured interviews that revealed the difficulties caregivers face in managing the home, more social and instrumental support services may be warranted. However, further inspection is needed given the modest size of effects in the quantitative analysis (0.38 points on the youth emotional difficulties 40-point scale). Employment was associated with more household hassles, thus these caregivers may require help to balance these new roles. Programs to help caregivers anticipate and plan for these changes may also be helpful. In addition, programs to aid caregivers to develop and maintain healthy social support networks, including those with other military spouses, may mitigate some of these stressors.

- **Target support toward those families reporting youth with elevated emotional difficulties and that experience more months of deployment.**

We noted that some youth in our study reported greater emotional difficulties (e.g., high and moderate difficulties) or elevated anxiety symptoms (meriting follow-up clinical assessment) during the study period, signifying that certain military youth may be struggling with problems that do not lessen with time or after return of the deployed parent. For example, youth who have experienced more cumulative months of parental deployment may require early intervention, particularly if they screen "high" for emotional difficulties. As of this writing, military organizations do not have systematic plans for screening and serving youth whose caregivers are experiencing significant months of deployment.

The findings also suggest that older teens (ages 15–17) and girls who are seeking a program like *Operation Purple*® may benefit from targeted initiatives within those programs. For example, older youth may need help adjusting to parental return or handling new home routines. Currently, many of the support programs focus on supporting younger youth (e.g., via Child Development Centers), with less programming for older teens. In addition, girls may need more support during the period of parental return to deal with the stress of parental relationships and mood changes. To date, the available programs have not been gender-specific, but the study findings suggest that some tailoring may be warranted.

- **Provide sufficient resources for caregiver support, particularly for Guard and Reserve caregivers.**

Finally, caregiver support to address emotional well-being is needed. The study findings show that caregivers applying to *Operation Purple*® were under strain in all facets of their lives, and while employment does appear to be associated with fewer emotional well-being issues, it is important to assist caregivers in juggling home and work responsibilities, particularly during the reintegration period. For Guard and Reserve caregivers, we should examine the availability of formal and informal mental health services, particularly when families are geographically far from military mental health providers or family support programs.

- **Focus programs on the quality of family communication.**

Finally, among our study participants, quality of family communication, specifically communication between caregivers and youth, was associated with how the family fared during and after deployment. Although we also examined the association between the frequency of communication and well-being outcomes, the perceived quality of the communication was more important than the frequency. Further, caregivers noted that communication quality with the deployed parent was related to challenges in their partner relationship. It may be important to consider integrating evidence-based strategies to improve the quality of caregiver-youth and caregiver-deployed parent communication in programs such as *Operation Purple*®. This may entail pre- and post-deployment interventions that address whole-family communication, focused on improving the perceived empathy for each family member's experience. It also may include strategies to help family members communicate better during potentially stressful times.

- **Implement support programs across the deployment cycle, including during the reintegration period.**

We noted that families applying to *Operation Purple*® faced challenges during deployment and reintegration, suggesting that support programs must be in place across the entire deployment cycle, at least for families seeking support via a one-week summer program such as *Operation Purple*®. Given the strong association between cumulative months of deployment and youth and caregiver difficulties, targeted initiatives for families experiencing many months of deployment may be needed. As a first step, it will be important to assess whether support resources are currently available throughout the reintegration period, not simply in the initial months of a first deployment or the initial month of redeployment. Further, we should assess whether families experiencing many months of deployment require additional or different interventions or support programs as the total months of parental absence accumulate. For example, these interventions may not include "what to expect from deployment" information but focus more on how to maintain a sense of family unity when a parent has been away for many months. Given that this sample was seeking services, it might be optimal to extend those supports past the camp period, engaging families through a deployment period.

In addition to these recommendations that specifically correspond to key factors, the next two suggestions relate to the study findings as a whole.

- **Consider screening for family emotional well-being.**

While significant attention has been paid to evaluating the mental health of service members, the examination of the well-being of youth and nondeployed caregivers applying to *Operation Purple*® suggests that at least some families may benefit from an ongoing assessment of family member health and well-being before and after a deployment. Given the significant relationship between caregiver emotional well-being and youth well-being in our study, as well as overall family challenges associated deployment, this type of screening, coupled with support provision, may be warranted. This assessment should include questions related to both difficulties and assets (e.g, coping strategies, existing support) to foster greater resilience.

The results also suggest a need for ongoing education of service providers, including teachers, pediatricians, and youth program leaders, specifically around youth social and emotional needs during and after deployment. The issues regarding elevated anxiety symptoms and emotional difficulties among our sample are critical and need to be addressed before problems worsen. Further, maintaining the health of those youth who are not "high risk" is important. School and primary care settings may offer opportunities to identify problems and deliver early, evidence-based intervention and prevention programs.

- **Require evaluation of programs in light of existing research.**

Over the past several years, there has been a rapid proliferation of programs to support military families. These programs have been initiated across the Department of Defense, the Services, as well as in the nongovernmental civilian sectors in an effort to support all military families, but especially those who experience deployment. These efforts have gone forward without much research guiding their content. Driven by the demand to provide support programs, family readiness groups and other organizations have mobilized to deliver a wide array of programs. To date, there has been no systematic assessment of the type, nature, and quality of these programs. As such, a rigorous and systematic evaluation of the current programs, particularly in light of this research, is needed. This evaluation should include an assessment of how well the program content aligns with the needs of the subgroups that would benefit most (e.g. those experiencing many months of deployment) and an outcomes-oriented analysis of program efficacy and effectiveness. Program attention should also be directed to the reintegration period. This study shows that adjustment is problematic, particularly for families that have experienced many deployments. However, their program needs may step beyond the usual education sessions useful for first-deployment families and extend months following service member homecoming.

Research Implications

While this study offers many new insights into the effects of deployment among a sample of military youth and caregivers, the study also highlights areas for future research. These research directions would address some of the inherent study limitations articulated in Chapter Two, and would also move the field of military family research forward by providing more detail into the youth and caregiver experience.

- **Compare military families with civilian cohorts.**

In this study, we noted that military youth in the study sample were experiencing greater emotional difficulties and elevated anxiety symptoms relative to the general U.S. youth population. However, we were only able to compare these data to available U.S. norms or population-based data, some of which have not been collected for five to ten years. Because we do not know the extent to which the study sample is representative of the general population of military youth, it is still important to compare military youth in a more representative sample with civilian youth. Given the stressors that all youth face currently with the economic downturn and other societal issues (APA, 2007), it is important to understand how a contemporary cohort of youth is faring in order to isolate the unique stress that deployment may contribute. Future studies of this nature should consider including appropriately matched samples of non-deploying civilian youth.

- **Examine caregiver well-being, with more measures of mental health.**

The emotional well-being of the nondeployed caregiver emerged as a significant factor in this research. However, we only used one short scale of mental health functioning (Mental Health Index), and did not employ diagnostic or clinical scales to assess for probable mental health disorders, such as items to assess for clinical depression or anxiety. Given the salience of this factor in the study as a characteristic of which families were facing more deployment-related challenges, further examination of the mental health and well-being of these caregivers may be warranted, using validated mental health screening tools.

In addition to mental health assessment, the qualitative analyses of caregiver difficulties suggests that further examination of the stressors in their life, how they cope, and which strategies are most useful would be valuable.

- **Anchor longitudinal timeline to deployment period, for baseline comparability.**

In this study, we were able to relate current deployment status as well as prior deployment history to the challenges that families in the study confronted. As summarized in Chapters Three and Four, we did attempt to compare the prospective experiences of those youth in the study who had a deployment at baseline and those who did not, as well as those youth in the study who experienced a deployed parent return during study period (post baseline). In most cases (with the exception of "high risk" youth for emotional difficulties), there were no significant differences between the groups, but this may be due to available sample size in each group.

However, because we sampled from a diverse applicant pool by deployment experience, we were unable to anchor all families to a specific deployment period (i.e., surveying all families at baseline before a deployment and following them through a deployment cycle). While we accounted for study period deployment status, we had fewer families experiencing the same deployment patterns at the time of the study upon which to draw many comparisons. Further, the first survey (baseline) was not conducted before a deployment for all families.

A study that anchors all families to a deployment period to allow assessment before a deployment would improve measurement of the effects associated specifically with deployment and could identify variables that may predict subsequent difficulties.

- **Follow youth over a longer period, into adulthood.**

Finally, we were able to follow families for one year (across three time points). We noted some modest changes in reported difficulties among our study sample over this study period; however, we do not know how these effects will change over a longer period of time for the population or even for a more representative sample of youth. Following youth over a longer time period will help to determine if the emotional difficulties we noted in this study worsen as deployments continue or if they level off. Tracking these youth into adulthood will also provide an opportunity to assess whether deployment-related challenges have an impact after adolescence.

Report Conclusions

The unique features of the current conflicts in Afghanistan and Iraq—including extended and repeated deployments, high levels of exposure to bodily harm among both combat and support personnel, and the extensive use of National Guard and Reserve forces—are creating psychological and emotional challenges for both service members and their families. This research represents an important step in understanding the nature of that impact for a sample of military youth and their nondeployed caregivers. Particularly for a service-seeking population, this study highlights ways to target and shape the content of the current set of support programs. It identifies key factors that may place members of military families at greater risk for behavioral and emotional difficulties and explores their consequences. Continuing to broaden and deepen understanding of this population with other samples of military youth, the challenges they face, and the resiliency resources they draw on in response will be critical for helping military organizations understand their needs and to respond appropriately.

APPENDIX A

Baseline Sample Recruitment: Additional Detail

This appendix provides additional information about how youth and caregivers were sampled and recruited for the study.

In 2008, approximately 12,500 youth applied to attend an *Operation Purple®* camp, and 9,138 youth with and without parental deployment experience were selected. Of the applicant pool, 4,674 families with youth between 11 and 17 years of age were eligible for the study. A single youth from families with more than one youth in the study age group was randomly selected to participate in the study. This resulted in a pool of 4,170, all of whom were sent a letter explaining the next steps and giving them the opportunity to opt out. Telephone calls were then made to landline telephone numbers listed on the camp applications by Abt-SRBI, a survey house contracted to conduct the interviews. Due to cell phone marketing restrictions, families that listed only cell phones were included if they contacted Abt-SRBI via the toll-free number provided in the prenotification letter, if caregivers contacted the project principal investigators, or if Abt-SRBI was able to locate them via publicly available landline numbers using a phone number search service. Based on these criteria, we determined that 3,165 families were eligible to participate.

Families were contacted between June 2008 and August 2008 in "batches," based on the youth's camp start date. The sampling plan was designed to be proportionate to deployed force composition across Army, Navy, Marines, and Air Force Active and Guard/Reserve service members (see Table 2.4). Abt-SRBI called families and spoke with the selected youth's primary caregiver, or home caregiver (HCG). *Primary caregiver* is defined as the caretaker responsible for the youth at present or when the deployed parent is away. Contact was made with 1,697 families (53.6 percent of the viable sample). Of those, 89 percent of households were screened and agreed to participate (n=1,507). Of the 3,165 viable samples, 196 opted out and 1,272 did not have a valid phone number and either were not called or were never reached.

Figure A.1 provides additional detail on the baseline sample flow.

Figure A.1
Recruitment Flow for Study Sample at Baseline Survey

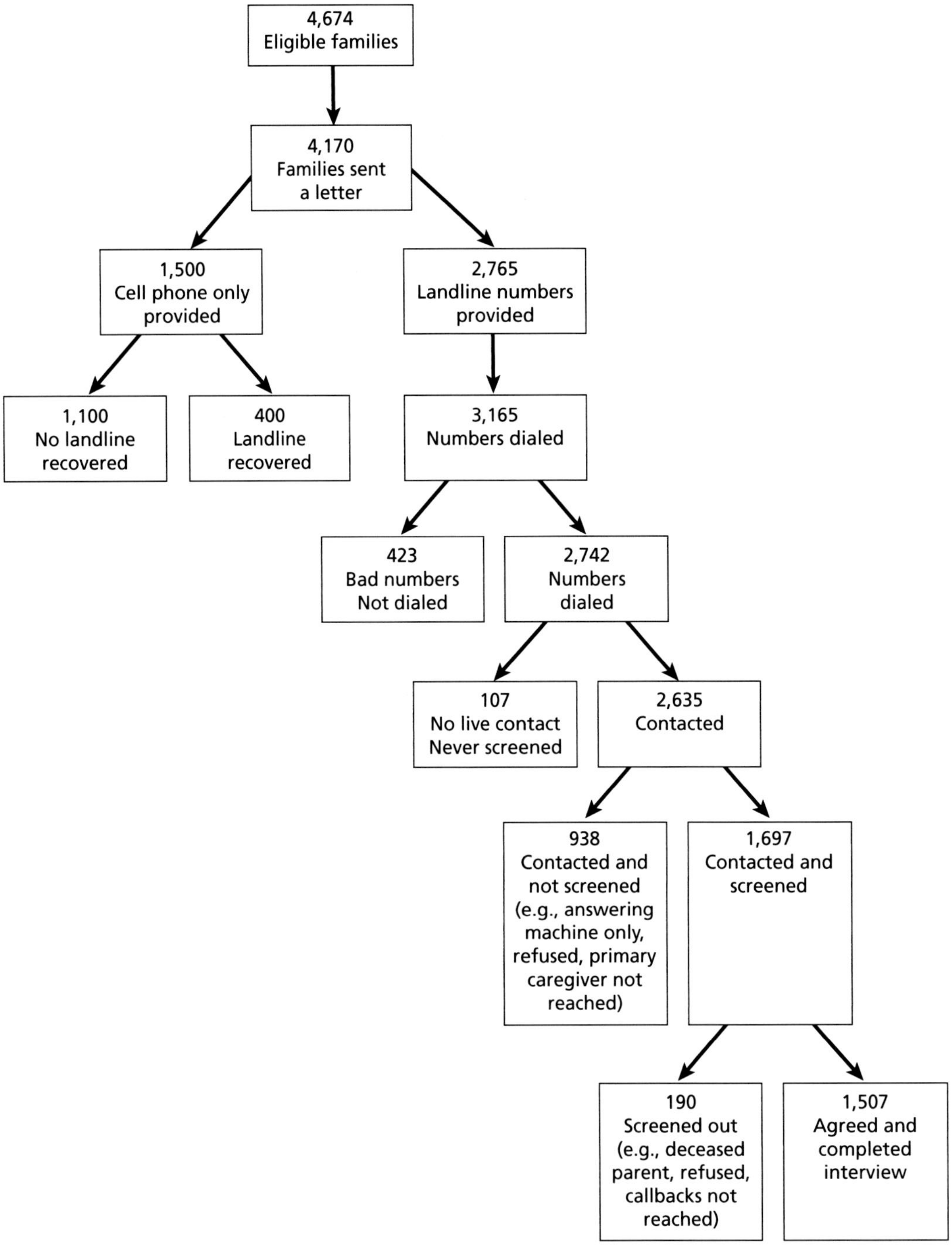

RAND *TR913-A.1*

APPENDIX B

Measures

This appendix provides detailed information about the measures used in this study by construct/domain. In Table B.1, we provide information about each measure, including the citation and psychometric properties.

Table B.1
Information on Measures

Construct/Domain	Respondent	Measure, Citation, and Modifications	Psychometrics
Youth and Maternal Well-Being			
Total emotional difficulties	HCG, youth	The Strengths and Difficulties Questionnaire (SDQ)(Goodman, 2001). The SDQ is a brief behavioral screening questionnaire made up of 25 items between 5 scales of 5 items each, generalizing scores for conduct problems, hyperactivity, emotional symptoms, peer problems, and prosocial behavior; all but the last scale are summed to generate a total difficulties score.	Range 0–40 (HCG: Cronbach's alpha = .77; Youth: Cronbach's alpha = .79)
Anxiety symptoms	Youth	Screen for Child Anxiety Related Emotional Disorders (SCARED; Birmaher et al., 1999). This short form of the SCARED is a 5-item measure that assesses children's anxiety symptoms.	Range 0–10; a higher number indicated more difficulties. (Cronbach's alpha = .80)
Peer functioning	HCG	Items are based on the Pediatric Quality of Life Inventory (PedsQL) Parent Report for Teens 4.0. The adapted scale was created by the Teen Depression Awareness Project (TDAP) (Jaycox, 2009). TDAP dropped two items from the PedsQL social subscale and modified the response set from "never . . . always" to "none of the time . . . all of the time" to be consistent with other survey scales. The stem was also modified accordingly to ask how "often" instead of how "much" things were a problem. The new three items scale assessed youths' ability to interact with other youth and had good internal consistency.	Range 0–12 (Cronbach's alpha = .79)

Table B.1—Continued

Construct/Domain	Respondent	Measure, Citation, and Modifications	Psychometrics
Family functioning	HCG	A 4-item scale created for the TDAP was used to assess youths' ability to get along in the family. The four items were modeled after PedsQL.	Range 0–16 (Cronbach's alpha = .78)
Academic Engagement	Youth	Academic Engagement (Rosenthal and Feldman, 1991) was determined using a 6-item scale that asks youth about being late to school, being ready for class, and other related items. The scale is based on a 5-point scale ranging from "none of the time" to "all of the time."	Range 0-24; a higher number indicated more difficulties. (Cronbach's alpha = .79)
School connectedness	Youth	This school connectedness scale consists of 5 items that assess the degree to which adolescents feel connected to their school, with items such as "I feel close to people at this school," and "I feel safe in this school (Resnick et al., 1997; You et al., 2008).	Range 0–20 (Cronbach's alpha = .81)
Problem behaviors	Youth	Problem Behavior Frequency Scale (PBFS; Farrell et al., 2000). The PBFS assess youths' problem behaviors in the past six months and is scored based on the number of times the behavior is reported from "never" to "20 or more times." Youth 11 to 14 were not asked about substance use and use of a weapon to hurt others.	Range 0–80; a higher number indicated more difficulties. (Cronbach's alpha = .81)
Maternal emotional well-being	HCG	Mental Health Index (MHI-5) (Berwick, 1991) is a well-validated and reliable measure of mental health. The MHI-5 is scored using a 5-point scale from "all of the time" to "none of the time."	Range 0–20 (Cronbach's alpha = .79)
Household hassles	HCG	This 7-item scale is based on a shortened version (15 items) of the Hall, Williams, and Greenberg (1985) inventory of daily hassles. Hassles include "having too many responsibilities" and "not enough time to do the things you want to do." The items are scored using a 4-point scale from "not bothered" to "bothered a great deal."	Range 7–28 (Cronbach's alpha = .79)
Relationship hassles	HCG	Like the household hassles scale above, this 4-item scale on relationship hassles is based on the Hall et al. (1985) shortened measure on daily hassles. The items are scored using a 4-point scale from "not bothered" to "bothered a great deal."	Range 4–16 (Cronbach's alpha = .79)
Parenting hassles	HCG	This scale is also based on Hall et al. (1985). The scale is made up of three items on parenting challenges, such as disagreements with others over discipline of the target youth and problems with the youth's behavior. The items are scored using a 4-point scale from "not bothered" to "bothered a great deal."	Range 3–12 (Cronbach's alpha = .79)

Table B.1—Continued

Construct/Domain	Respondent	Measure, Citation, and Modifications	Psychometrics
Youth report of parent communication	Youth	The youth communication scale is also based on the Pittsburgh Youth study and is made up of 5 items, such as "Is your (HCG) a good listener?" Youth respond using a 5-point scale from "almost always" to "not at all." One item was reverse coded and then all five items were summed. Again, scores are inverted so that higher score indicates more communication problems.	Range 0–20 (Cronbach's alpha = .80)
Parent communication scale	HCG	This 6-item scale on parent communication is based on the Pittsburgh Youth Study (Thornberry, Huizinga, and Loeber, 1995; Loeber and Stouthamer-Loeber, 1998). Parents respond using a 3-point (0,1,2) scale from "almost never" to "almost always" to questions such as "Do you discuss child-related problems with your child?" Scores are based on summed items. For this study, scores are inverted so that higher scores represent more communication problems. The scale has good internal consistency and differentiates between community and high-risk samples.	Range 0–12 (Cronbach's alpha = .80)
Deployment-Related Experiences[a]			
Recent deployment	HCG	There are three variables defined for the year prior to the study period (Summer 2007–Summer 2008). We calculated the total months of deployment in the year prior to the study period and whether the youth experienced a deployment or return during that pre-study period.	Except for the deployment months (0–12) in the year prior to study year, all others are dichotomous
Study period deployment	HCG	There are three variables defined during the study period. We included variables related to whether the youth experienced a deployment and/or a parental return *during* the study period. We also included a real-time deployment indicator to note whether a parent was deployed at each survey wave.	All are dichotomous
Cumulative deployment	HCG	This included the total months of deployment from 2001 to the start of the study period (Summer 2008) and the total number of deployments during that same period.	Three levels: no deployment, less than 1 year, and more than one year (13+ months) cumulative deployment
Deployment location	HCG	We also noted if at least one of the deployments before the study period were to Iraq or Afghanistan versus all other locations.	Dichotomous: Iraq and Afghanistan versus others

Table B.1—Continued

Construct/Domain	Respondent	Measure, Citation, and Modifications	Psychometrics
Youth difficulties with deployment (during deployment)	HCG, youth	New scale was created using confirmatory factor analysis that treated individual items categorically. Many of these deployment experience items were developed as a result of a pilot analysis of *Operation Purple®* participants (Chandra et al., 2008). The measures were reviewed by military family researchers and National Military Family Association program leaders for face and content validity. The HCG and youth scales ask about difficulties the youth experienced during deployment (e.g., "dealing with life without his/her deployed parent"). The HCG scale is made up of 10 items. The youth scale includes 9 items. Both scales are dichotomized (yes/no).	HCG: scale range 0–10 (Cronbach's alpha = .79) Youth: scale range 0–9 (Cronbach's alpha = .79)
Youth difficulties with reintegration (post deployment)	HCG, youth	As indicated above, new scales were created for this study. The HCG and youth scales ask questions about difficulties with reintegration (after the deployed parent returns), such as "getting to know his/her deployed parent again." Both scales made up of 6 items, with responses dichotomized (yes/no).	HCG: scale range 0–6 (Cronbach's alpha = .79) Youth: scale range 0–6 (Cronbach's alpha = .80)
Caregiver difficulties with deployment: Concerns about community support, other concerns during deployment (e.g., parenting)	HCG	This deployment scale was initially made up of 9 items based on a newly developed measure. The scale was reduced to two 4-item scales based on confirmatory factor analysis and labeled "concerns about community support" and "other deployment concerns." Caregivers were asked whether or not they experienced problems related to the amount of access and community support they received during a deployment. The other scale contained 4 items and focused on parenting issues. Responses were dichotomized (yes/no).	Both scales: range 0–4 (Cronbach's alpha = .85)

[a] A higher score indicates more difficulties/problems for all scales.

Technical Details for Quantitative Analyses

This appendix provides additional technical details on the statistical approaches used in the quantitative analyses of the survey data.

In this study we applied a set of general linear mixed models (McCulloch and Searle, 2001) to estimate the relationship between the outcomes of interest and key predictors while accounting for relevant covariates. In these models, we have taken into consideration the natural change in the outcomes across time points, i.e., trajectory, as well as correlations among repeated measurements within each survey respondent. We used the PROC MIXED in the general statistical software package SAS 9 (SAS Institute Inc., 2002–2004) to fit the mixed model. The linear mixed model has the following form:

$$Y_{it} = \mathbf{X}_i\boldsymbol{\beta} + \mathbf{Z}_{it}\boldsymbol{\gamma} + a_i + e_{it},$$

where Y_{it} is the outcome of individual i at time t, t = 0,1,2. The right-hand side consists of four parts: the effect of time-invariant factors $\mathbf{X}_i\boldsymbol{\beta}$, the effect of time-varying factors $\mathbf{Z}_{it}\boldsymbol{\gamma}$, an individual-level random effect a_i, and the independent error term e_{it}. Both $\mathbf{X}_i$ and $\mathbf{Z}_{it}$ are vectors consisting of multiple predictors. A predictor belongs to $\mathbf{X}_i$ if its value does not change across time points for the same individual, e.g., the gender of the youth. Most covariates in the study fall in this category. Some variables may change across time points, such as the service component and rank of the parent in military. However, during the relatively short study period, these variables usually did not change and are still considered time-invariant. Time-varying predictors are usually the "real-time" measurements, e.g., whether a parent is deployed at the survey time, the communication difficulty between a caregiver and youth at the survey time. The time of survey is a special time-varying predictor. Over the study period, some outcomes may experience a natural change across time points. This natural growth trend, if ignored, may negatively affect the statistical inference. Therefore, we explicitly used time indicators as time-varying predictors. Specifically, we created two dummy variables to represent the second and third survey waves. This approach is suitable for studies with sparse and few time points. This allows for a totally flexible trajectory. Besides the natural time trend, recent deployment events may change the shape of the trajectories. To account for such potential influences, we further include two interactions terms between time and deployment variables defined in the study period.

We used a comprehensive list of variables describing the family background, deployment characteristics, the caregiver's own problems, and the communications between caregivers and youth. Depending on the outcome, $\mathbf{X}_i$ or $\mathbf{Z}_{it}$ may include or exclude some predictor(s). A qualitative predictor with m levels, e.g., service branch in the military, is represented by m–1 dummy variables. One level is chosen as the baseline level. The combination of all baseline levels is the intercept in the linear model and is contained in $\mathbf{X}_i$. The choice of the reference level does not affect the statistical inference based on the type III F-test.

The role of the random effect a_i is two-fold. First, it is an individual-level effect, independent of all predictors. Therefore, it allows for heterogeneity in the population due to unobserved factors, i.e., not included in $\mathbf{X}_i$ or $\mathbf{Z}_{it}$. Second, a_i is normally distributed with an unknown variance, which explicitly indicates Y_{i1}, Y_{i2}, and Y_{i3} are correlated measurements.

There are two types of tests to examine the statistical significance of a predictor. First, one can test whether a single entry of the coefficient vectors $\boldsymbol{\beta}$ or $\boldsymbol{\gamma}$ is equal to 0 by the regular *t*-test. The *t*-statistic is equal to the point estimates divided by its standard error. P-values are calculated using a *t* distribution with d.f. equal to the error d.f. The *t*-tests can depend on the choice of the reference level, i.e., the definition of the intercept. The second approach is the type III F-test in SAS, or more formally, the general linear hypothesis test. The construction of the F-test involves more technical discussions and is omitted here. The F-test can simultaneously test multivariate relationships among several entries of the $\boldsymbol{\beta}$ or $\boldsymbol{\gamma}$. For a predictor with degrees of freedom (d.f. 1), the F-test and *t*-test give identical results. Since both continuous predictors (e.g., age and deployment counts) and binary predictors (e.g., gender, service type, and some deployment status variables) have d.f. 1, we can use either test for these predictors. In testing qualitative predictors with $m>2$ levels, there will be $m-1$ *t*-tests comparing a level with the reference level. It is not clear when a factor can be considered influential based on multiple *t*-tests. One may tentatively claim influential if at least one *t*-test is significant. However, such a decision rule lacks rigorous statistical justification. Nevertheless, the F-test can examine any deviation from an all-equivalent relationship among the *p* levels of a qualitative factor. Hence, the F-test yields an unambiguous conclusion for the overall significance of a qualitative predictor. In this study, we conducted both types of tests for the qualitative predictors with multiple levels. We used the F-test to examine the overall effect of a qualitative predictor. If the F-test rejects the null hypothesis we claim that this predictor has a significant main effect. The details of the differential effects among all *m* levels are revealed by the follow-up *t*-tests for pairwise comparisons.

We use caregiver-reported SDQ to illustrate the specific details of the linear mixed model. For simplicity in presentation,we use bold notation, $\boldsymbol{\beta}$ () and $\boldsymbol{\gamma}$ (), to denote the coefficient vectors corresponding to a categorical factor with more than two levels.

$$
\begin{aligned}
SDQ_{it} = {} & \text{intercept} + \boldsymbol{\beta}\ (\text{race}) + \beta\ (\text{female caregiver}) + \beta\ (\text{girl}) + \boldsymbol{\beta}\ (\text{rank}) + \\
& \boldsymbol{\beta}(\text{branch}) + \beta\ (\text{component}) + \beta\ (\text{caregiver employment}) + \\
& \boldsymbol{\beta}(\text{housing status}) + \beta\ (\text{camp attendance}) + \\
& \beta_1 \times \text{youth age at baseline} + \beta_2 \times \text{caregiver age at baseline} + \\
& \boldsymbol{\beta}\ (\text{levels of months deployed during 2001 to baseline}) + \\
& \beta\ (\text{deployed during study period}) + \\
& \beta\ (\text{returned during study period}) + \\
& \beta\ (\text{deployed during year before study period}) + \\
& \beta\ (\text{returned from deployment during year before study period}) + \\
& \beta_3 \times \text{number of months deployed during year before study period} + \\
& \beta\ (\text{deployment location}) + \\
& \boldsymbol{\gamma}\ (\text{time}) + \gamma\ (\text{real-time deployment}) + \\
& \boldsymbol{\gamma}\ (\text{time} \times \text{deployed during study period}) +
\end{aligned}
$$

γ (time × returned during study period) +
γ_1 × number of deployments + γ_2 × caregiver's own SDQ_{it} +
γ_3 × caregiver's $MHI\text{-}5_{it}$.

As discussed in Chapter Two, subgroups are defined based on the deployment characteristics. Testing the time-invariant effects, such as β (levels of months deployed during 2001 to baseline) and β (deployed during study period), reveals the potential differences in intercepts of the trajectories among subgroups. The overall F-test for γ (time) can reveal whether the trajectory is flat for the reference group (as represented by the intercept). The overall F-tests for γ (time × deployed during study period) and γ (time × returned during study period) further reveal whether the trajectories are different among the subgroups. Predicted values used for plotting the trajectories in Chapter Three are best linear unbiased predictions combining all the time-invariant and time-varying effects, which take the corresponding values of the subgroup.

Plots of the trajectories in Chapter Three are based on the least-square estimates of the mixed model. The main differences among the trajectories are based on the inference for the deployment characteristic in the study year, which is used to define these subgroups. The trajectories may still have true differences due to their secondary difference in other covariates, which are at least marginally significant in the mixed model. For example, in the above model the recent year deployment experience differs slightly, and a time-varying covariate of the caregiver (caregiver emotional health) also differs significantly, among the three groups. These contributed to the visual difference in the plot. However, the mixed model suggests that if these covariates are controlled at the same level, then the three groups do not have difference.

Specifically, we used one group at time = 0 as the reference point. We used least-square estimation for the reference point. The remaining eight points are located with respect to the reference point, using the corresponding characteristics, e.g., average deployment months in recent year, predicted caregiver's MHI-5 at time = 1, etc. We did not use insignificant covariates since their big standard errors severely distort the plot. For Figure 3.2, the blue line (the subgroup of deployed and returned) has roughly 2.5 more deployment months in the recent year and 1.3 points higher in MHI-5 than the other two groups, which result in a difference of roughly 0.8 points between the blue line and the others.

Multiple Comparisons

This study is based on the previous cross-sectional analysis (Chandra et al., 2010a), which explores the potentially influential factors for the outcomes of interest. The current longitudinal analysis can remove the heterogeneity among survey respondents and yield inference for the authentic associations between outcomes and factors. Hence, this longitudinal analysis is intended to confirm the preliminary findings from the first stage. The longitudinal study is also focused on a small number of previously identified factors. Therefore, this longitudinal study is a confirmatory study.

It is helpful to first review the effort of multiplicity adjustment in the previous analysis (Chandra et al., 2010), which involved about 800 *t*-tests based on multiple regression models. We applied both the conservative Bonferroni adjustment and the more recent Benjamini-Hochberg linear step-up method. We also considered three scopes of adjustments: pooling all tests together, pooling tests by categories of outcomes, and pooling tests by each outcome. Hence, we had a total of six schemes to adjust multiple comparisons. These six schemes yielded very similar results. This is perhaps due to the lack of moderate signals (in the sense of multiple comparisons but the classic effect size). We finally chose the scheme of Bonforroni adjustment and pooling within each outcome.

We do not need multiplicity adjustment if we only focus on a small number of hypotheses and/or a few specific hypotheses. In the current longitudinal analysis, the goal is to confirm the previous findings. Essentially, we aim to examine a special subset of two or three hypotheses for each outcome. The issue of multiplicity is no longer a legitimate concern. For example, if the interest is focused on the parent's MHI-5, testing it alone or together with 10,000 other factors without adjustment does not make a difference. It is true that without adjustments we will make many false findings. However, the chance that MHI-5 is among the false findings is still .05.

Based on these considerations, p=.05 for previously discovered factors such as deployment length/parent MHI-5/youth gender is adequate evidence for significance in the longitudinal study, since it confirms the previous findings. However, for variables that were new to this analysis (primarily the communication items), we still applied the strict Bonferroni adjustment.

Sensitivity Analysis Based on Multiple Imputation

Multiple imputation (MI) is a popular approach to missing data under the missing-at-random assumption. The MI method generates multiple samples from the prediction distribution of missing data. These samples would be different from each other since they are randomly generated and none of them can equal the estimated mean (predicted value) exactly. Usually, identical analyses are conducted for each imputed dataset. A model-averaging step, usually in the form of weighted average of point estimates, is taken to combine the results. Most MI methods still require that only a small part of the data is missing.

In this report, we used a linear mixed model to estimate various associations. We applied the MI analysis to examine the potential sensitivity of the main results to the missing data. We assessed the similarities between the two sets of analyses by comparing the significant findings both with and without adjustments for multiple comparisons. We considered the results similar because these two approaches generally had significant findings in common. The differences between these two sets of analyses are mainly in the specific values of the estimates and associated standard deviations, which is a common phenomenon when an alternative technical approach is used instead.

APPENDIX D

Youth Tables

This appendix provides detailed data tables for the survey findings related to the youth outcomes. These findings are discussed in more detail in Chapter Three. Numbers in parentheses are standard deviations.

Table D.1
Youth Outcomes (Anxiety and Emotional Difficulties)

		Youth-Reported		Caregiver-Reported
		Anxiety Symptoms	**Emotional Difficulties**	**Emotional Difficulties**
Intercept		2.99 (0.6)+++	12.82 (2.1)+++	9.24 (2.29)+++
Data-collection phase (time)	Baseline (0)	0.26 (0.08)+++***	1.61 (0.22)+++***	0.84 (0.2)+++***
	First follow-up (1)	−0.02 (0.08)***	0.37 (0.22)***	−0.59 (0.2)++***
	Second follow-up (2)	—	—	—
Military Characteristics				
Deployed parent rank	Junior enlisted (E1–E4)	0.15 (0.22)	0.62 (0.76)*	1.03 (0.83)*
	Mid-grade enlisted	0.02 (0.12)	0.45 (0.41)*	0.86 (0.45)*
	Officer (O/W)	−0.2 (0.12)	−0.78 (0.42)*	−0.45 (0.46)*
	Senior enlisted (E7–E9)	—	—	—
Deployed parent branch	Air Force	−0.38 (0.16)+	−0.92 (0.55)	−1.63 (0.6)++
	Army	−0.1 (0.15)	−0.16 (0.51)	−0.93 (0.56)
	Marines	−0.16 (0.24)	−0.6 (0.83)	−0.83 (0.91)
	Navy	—	—	—
Deployed parent component	Active	0.06 (0.11)	0.35 (0.38)	−0.35 (0.41)
	Reserve/National Guard	—	—	—
Youth and Caregiver Characteristics				
Race	Multiracial/other	−0.1 (0.15)	−0.09 (0.54)	0.44 (0.59)
	Black, non-Hispanic	−0.02 (0.16)	0.02 (0.56)	−0.77 (0.61)
	Hispanic	0.26 (0.21)	0.49 (0.74)	−0.26 (0.81)
	White, non-Hispanic	—	—	—

Table D.1—Continued

		Youth-Reported		Caregiver-Reported
		Anxiety Symptoms	Emotional Difficulties	Emotional Difficulties
Youth age		−0.1 (0.03)++***	−0.19 (0.11)	−0.23 (0.12)
Youth gender	Female	0.64 (0.09)+++***	−0.08 (0.32)	−1.78 (0.35)+++***
	Male	—	—	—
Operation Purple® attendance	Yes	0 (0.11)	−0.4 (0.37)	0.09 (0.41)
	No	—	—	—
Caregiver age		0.01 (0.01)	−0.03 (0.03)	0.02 (0.03)
Caregiver gender	Female	−0.41 (0.22)	−1.18 (0.75)	0.84 (0.82)
	Male	—	—	—
Caregiver employed	Employed outside home	−0.02 (0.07)	−0.29 (0.22)	−0.3 (0.22)
	Not employed outside home	—	—	—
Caregiver report of own emotional well-being (MHI-5)		0.02 (0.01)+*	0.12 (0.03)+++***	0.38 (0.03)+++***
Caregiver–youth communication quality (youth report)		0.02 (0.01)+*	0.3 (0.03)+++***	0.07 (0.03)+*
Housing	Military (on- or off-base)	−0.11 (0.13)	−0.16 (0.4)	0.17 (0.39)
	Own home	−0.18 (0.12)	0.27 (0.35)	0.57 (0.35)
	Rent, with family, or other	—	—	—
Deployment Experience				
Real-time deployment flag		−0.05 (0.09)	−0.28 (0.25)	−0.13 (0.23)
Deployed during study period	Yes	0.11 (0.2)	−0.18 (0.64)	−1.12 (0.66)
	No	—	—	—
Returned during study period	Yes	−0.24 (0.21)	−0.53 (0.68)	−0.33 (0.71)
	No	—	—	—
Deployed during year before study period	Yes	0.18 (0.2)	1.06 (0.69)	−0.68 (0.75)
	No	—	—	—
Returned from deployment during year before study period	Yes	−0.14 (0.15)	−0.69 (0.51)	−0.16 (0.56)
Deployed during year before study period	Yes	0.18 (0.2)	1.06 (0.69)	−0.68 (0.75)
	No	—	—	—
Returned from deployment during year before study period	Yes	−0.14 (0.15)	−0.69 (0.51)	−0.16 (0.56)
	No	—	—	—

Table D.1—Continued

		Youth-Reported		Caregiver-Reported
		Anxiety Symptoms	Emotional Difficulties	Emotional Difficulties
Months deployed during year before study period		0.01 (0.02)	0.01 (0.06)	0.16 (0.07)+*
Months deployed (2001 to baseline)	1–12 months	−0.11 (0.19)	−0.09 (0.65)	−0.14 (0.71)
	12+ months	0.11 (0.21)	0.26 (0.73)	0.47 (0.8)
	Never	—	—	—
Total number of deployments (2001 to baseline)		−0.06 (0.04)	−0.07 (0.14)	0.1 (0.15)
Deployment location	At least one deployment in Iraq/Afghanistan	−0.07 (0.13)	0.36 (0.44)	0.18 (0.48)
	No deployment in Iraq/Afghanistan	—	—	—
Interaction between deployment during year before study period and time of data collection	Deploy & time=0	−0.26 (0.18)	−0.95 (0.51)	−0.23 (0.48)
	Deploy & time=1	−0.06 (0.17)	−0.66 (0.49)	0.67 (0.45)
	Deploy & time=2	—	—	—
	No deploy & time=0	—	—	—
	No deploy & time=1	—	—	—
	No deploy & time=2	—	—	—
Interaction between return from deployment during year before study period and time of data collection	Return & time=0	0.25 (0.22)	0.97 (0.62)	1.09 (0.58)
	Return & time=1	0.14 (0.18)	0.86 (0.52)	0.48 (0.48)
	Return & time=2	—	—	—
	No return & time=0	—	—	—
	No return & time=1	—	—	—
	No return & time=2	—	—	—

* .05-level F-test.

** 01-level F-test.

*** .001-level F-test.

+. 05-level *t*-test.

++ .01-level *t*-test.

+++ .001-level *t*-test.

Table D.2
Youth Outcomes (Peer, Family Functioning, Academic and Risk Behaviors)

		Youth-Reported		Caregiver-Reported	
		Academic Engagement Problems	Problem Behaviors	Peer Functioning Problems	Family Functioning Problems
Intercept		0.39 (1.06)	−0.94 (2.41)	3.36 (0.77)+++	2.52 (0.99)+
Data-collection phase (time)	Baseline (0)	0.03 (0.14)**	0.42 (0.32)	0.16 (0.1)***	0.15 (0.14)*
	First follow-up (1)	−0.36 (0.14)+**	0.15 (0.32)	0.19 (0.1)+***	−0.05 (0.14)*
	Second follow-up (2)	—	—	—	—
Military Characteristics					
Deployed parent rank	Junior enlisted (E1–E4)	0.75 (0.38)+**	0.44 (0.87)	0.02 (0.28)	0.45 (0.35)
	Mid-grade enlisted	0.12 (0.2)**	0.20 (0.47)	0.16 (0.15)	0.23 (0.19)
	Officer (O/W)	−0.4 (0.21)**	0.37 (0.48)	−0.12 (0.15)	0.23 (0.2)
	Senior enlisted (E7–E9)	—	—	—	—
Deployed parent branch	Air Force	0.12 (0.27)	0.31 (0.63)	−0.43 (0.2)+	−0.26 (0.26)
	Army	−0.22 (0.25)	0.52 (0.58)	−0.31 (0.19)	−0.17 (0.24)
	Marines	−0.66 (0.41)	0.01 (0.95)	−0.07 (0.3)	0.15 (0.39)
	Navy	—	—	—	—
Deployed parent component	Active	0.16 (0.19)	0.46 (0.44)	−0.26 (0.14)	−0.35 (0.18)
	Reserve/ National Guard	—	—	—	—
Youth and Caregiver Characteristics					
Race	Multiracial/ other	0.38 (0.27)***	1.22 (0.61)+*	−0.06 (0.2)	0.1 (0.25)
	Black, non-Hispanic	1.14 (0.28)+++***	1.34 (0.64)+*	−0.24 (0.2)	−0.22 (0.26)
	Hispanic	0.66 (0.37)***	−0.20 (0.85)	−0.29 (0.27)	−0.28 (0.35)
	White, non-Hispanic	—	—	—	—
Youth age		0.24 (0.05)+++***	0.26 (0.13)+*	−0.16 (0.04)+++***	−0.02 (0.05)
Youth gender	Female	−0.83 (0.16)+++***	-1.72(0.37)+++***	−0.2 (0.12)	−0.43 (0.15)++**
	Male	—	—	—	—
Operation Purple® attendance	Yes	−0.05 (0.18)	−0.61 (0.42)	−0.04 (0.14)	−0.19 (0.17)
	No	—	—	—	—
Caregiver age		0 (0.02)	−0.03 (0.04)	−0.01 (0.01)	0 (0.01)
Caregiver gender	Female	0.16 (0.37)	0.91 (0.86)	0.3 (0.27)	0.56 (0.35)
	Male	—	—	—	—
Caregiver employed	Employed outside home	0.04 (0.13)	0.27 (0.30)	−0.09 (0.09)	0.06 (0.12)

Table D.2—Continued

		Youth-Reported		Caregiver-Reported	
		Academic Engagement Problems	**Problem Behaviors**	**Peer Functioning Problems**	**Family Functioning Problems**
	Not employed outside home	—	—	—	—
Caregiver report of own emotional well-being (MHI-5)		0.06 (0.02)+++***	0.05 (0.04)	0.09 (0.01)+++***	0.22 (0.02)+++***
Caregiver-youth communication quality (youth report)		0.17 (0.02)+++***	0.32 (0.04)+++***	0.03 (0.01)+*	0.07 (0.02)+++***
Housing	Military (on- or off-base)	−0.12 (0.24)	0.39 (0.53)	0.16 (0.17)	0.12 (0.22)
	Own home	0 (0.21)	0.75 (0.46)	0.19 (0.14)	0.22 (0.19)
	Rent, with family, or other	—	—	—	—
Deployment Experience					
Real-time deployment flag		0.15 (0.16)	−0.18 (0.35)	−0.18 (0.11)	0.16 (0.15)
Deployed during study period	Yes	−0.19 (0.35)	1.03 (0.79)	−0.22 (0.25)	−0.39 (0.33)
	No	—	—	—	—
Returned during study period	Yes	−0.22 (0.37)	−1.19 (0.84)	−0.18 (0.26)	0.08 (0.35)
	No	—	—	—	—
Deployed during year before study period	Yes	0.86 (0.34)+	0.72 (0.78)	−0.18 (0.25)	−0.28 (0.32)
	No	—	—		
Returned from deployment during year before study period	Yes	−0.4 (0.25)	0.16 (0.58)	−0.04 (0.19)	0.12 (0.24)
	No	—	—	—	—
Months deployed during year before study period		−0.02 (0.03)	−0.05 (0.07)	0.04 (0.02)	0.03 (0.03)
Months deployed (2001 to baseline)	1–12 months	−0.28 (0.32)	0.33 (0.74)	0.09 (0.24)	−0.33 (0.3)
	13+ months	−0.09 (0.36)	0.75 (0.84)	0.14 (0.27)	−0.29 (0.34)
	Never	—	—	—	—
Total number of deployments (2001 to baseline)		−0.03 (0.07)	−0.01 (0.16)	-0.02 (0.05)	0.1 (0.06)
Deployment Location	At least one deployment in Iraq/Afghanistan	0.3 (0.22)	−0.18 (0.50)	−0.03 (0.16)	0.51 (0.2)+*

Table D.2—Continued

		Youth-Reported		Caregiver-Reported	
		Academic Engagement Problems	Problem Behaviors	Peer Functioning Problems	Family Functioning Problems
	No deployment in Iraq/ Afghanistan	—	—	—	—
Interaction between deployment during year before study period and time of data collection	Deploy & time=0	0.05 (0.33)	−1.22 (0.74)	0 (0.23)	0.41 (0.32)
	Deploy & time=1	0.27 (0.31)	−0.73 (0.70)	−0.12 (0.21)	0.24 (0.3)
	Deploy & time=2	—	—	—	—
	No deploy & time=0	—	—	—	—
	No deploy & time=1	—	—	—	—
	No deploy & time=2	—	—	—	—
Interaction between return from deployment during year before study period and time of data collection	Return & time=0	−0.26 (0.4)	0.79 (0.90)	0.61 (0.27)+	−0.23 (0.38)
	Return & time=1	−0.21 (0.33)	0.48 (0.74)	0.46 (0.23)+	−0.16 (0.32)
	Return & time=2	—	—	—	—
	No return & time=0	—	—	—	—
	No return & time=1	—	—	—	—
	No return & time=2	—	—	—	—

* .05-level F-test.

** 01-level F-test.

*** .001-level F-test.

+. .05-level *t*-test.

++ .01-level *t*-test.

+++ .001-level *t*-test.

Table D.3
Youth Deployment Outcomes

		Youth-Reported		Caregiver-Reported	
		Difficulties with Parental Deployment	Reintegration Concerns	Youth's Difficulties with Deployment	Youth's Difficulties with Reintegration
Intercept		1.22 (0.64)	0.77 (0.61)	0.03 (0.67)	0.2 (0.68)
Data-collection phase (time)	Baseline (0)	0.06 (0.09)*	0.07 (0.09)*	0.41 (0.1)+++**	−0.03 (0.09)
	First follow-up (1)	0.26 (0.16)*	0.35 (0.17)+*	0.09 (0.18)**	0.07 (0.15)
	Second follow-up (2)	—	—	—	—
Military Characteristics					
Deployed parent rank	Junior enlisted (E1–E4)	0.02 (0.23)	0.17 (0.22)	0.08 (0.24)	0.04 (0.26)
	Mid-grade enlisted	−0.16 (0.12)	0.07 (0.12)	0.04 (0.13)	0.05 (0.13)
	Officer (O/W)	−0.05 (0.13)	0 (0.12)	0.22 (0.13)	−0.04 (0.13)
	Senior enlisted (E7–E9)	—	—	—	—
Deployed parent branch	Air Force	−0.28 (0.17)**	−0.15 (0.16)	−0.11 (0.17)	0.32 (0.18)
	Army	0.06 (0.15)**	0.18 (0.15)	−0.18 (0.16)	0.22 (0.16)
	Marines	−0.57 (0.25)+**	0.04 (0.24)	0.24 (0.25)	0.47 (0.26)
	Navy	—	—	—	—
Deployed parent component	Active	0.07 (0.12)	−0.12 (0.11)	−0.45 (0.12)+++***	−0.25 (0.12)+*
	Reserve/ National Guard	—	—	—	—
Youth and Caregiver Characteristics					
Race	Multiracial/ other	0.15 (0.16)	0.34 (0.15)+**	0.22 (0.16)*	0.2 (0.17)
	Black, non-Hispanic	0.25 (0.17)	0.33 (0.16)+**	−0.3 (0.17)*	−0.02 (0.18)
	Hispanic	0.31 (0.22)	0.49 (0.21)+**	−0.51 (0.23)+*	−0.01 (0.24)
	White, non-Hispanic	—	—	—	—
Youth age		0.1 (0.03)++**	0.1 (0.03)++**	0.11 (0.03)++***	0.01 (0.03)
Youth gender	Female	0.41 (0.1)+++***	0.45 (0.09)+++***	−0.03 (0.1)	0.13 (0.1)
	Male	—	—	—	—

Table D.3—Continued

		Youth-Reported		Caregiver-Reported	
		Difficulties with Parental Deployment	Reintegration Concerns	Youth's Difficulties with Deployment	Youth's Difficulties with Reintegration
Operation Purple® attendance	Yes	0 (0.11)	–0.06 (0.11)	0.19 (0.12)	–0.05 (0.12)
	No	—	—	—	—
Caregiver age		–0.02 (0.01)	–0.02 (0.01)+*	–0.01 (0.01)	0 (0.01)
Caregiver gender	Female	–0.3 (0.23)	–0.27 (0.22)	0.29 (0.24)	0.37 (0.25)
	Male	—	—	—	—
Caregiver employed	Employed outside home	0.01 (0.08)	0.09 (0.08)	0.24 (0.09)++**	0.24 (0.09)++**
	Not employed outside home	—	—	—	—
Caregiver report of own emotional well-being (MHI-5)		0.01 (0.01)	0.01 (0.01)	0.07 (0.01)+++***	0.09 (0.01)+++***
Total emotional difficulties (caregiver SDQ)		0.05 (0.01)+++***	0.04 (0.01)+++***	0.15 (0.01)+++***	0.09 (0.01)+++***
Housing	Military (on- or off-base)	–0.16 (0.15)	0.07 (0.14)	–0.35 (0.15)+	–0.07 (0.15)
	Own home	–0.02 (0.13)	0.12 (0.13)	–0.28 (0.14)+	–0.11 (0.13)
	Rent, with family, or other	—	—	—	—
Deployment Experience					
Real-time deployment flag		–0.09 (0.1)	–0.42 (0.1)+++***	–0.26 (0.11)+*	–0.13 (0.1)
Deployed during study period	Yes	–0.13 (0.21)	0.04 (0.21)	0.4 (0.22)	0.31 (0.22)
	No	—	—	—	—
Returned during study period	Yes	–0.06 (0.22)	–0.12 (0.22)	–0.06 (0.23)	–0.2 (0.23)
	No	—	—	—	—
Deployed during year before study period	Yes	0.17 (0.2)	–0.13 (0.19)	0.09 (0.21)	–0.37 (0.21)
	No	—	—	—	—

Table D.3—Continued

		Youth-Reported		Caregiver-Reported	
		Difficulties with Parental Deployment	Reintegration Concerns	Youth's Difficulties with Deployment	Youth's Difficulties with Reintegration
Returned from deployment during year before study period	Yes	−0.3 (0.15)+*	0.19 (0.14)	0.05 (0.15)	0.25 (0.16)
	No	—	—	—	—
Months deployed during year before study period		0 (0.02)	0 (0.02)	−0.02 (0.02)	0.01 (0.02)
Months deployed (2001 to baseline)	1–12 months	0.1 (0.2)	0.36 (0.2)***	0.27 (0.21)*	0.25 (0.22)***
	13+ months	0.18 (0.23)	0.71 (0.22)+++***	0.54 (0.24)+*	0.75 (0.25)++***
	Never	—	—	—	—
Total number of deployments (2001 to baseline)		0 (0.04)	−0.02 (0.04)	0.05 (0.04)	0.04 (0.04)
Deployment location	At least one deployment in Iraq/ Afghanistan	0.07 (0.13)	−0.03 (0.12)	0.02 (0.13)	0.06 (0.14)
	No deployment in Iraq/ Afghanistan	—	—	—	—
Interaction between deployment during year before study period and time of data collection	Deploy & time=0	0.03 (0.21)	−0.12 (0.21)	−0.34 (0.23)	0.1 (0.2)
	Deploy & time=1	−0.2 (0.24)	−0.27 (0.24)	−0.08 (0.26)	−0.23 (0.24)
	Deploy & time=2	—	—	—	—
	No deploy & time=0	—	—	—	—
	No deploy & time=1	—	—	—	—
	No deploy & time=2	—	—	—	—

Table D.3—Continued

		Youth-Reported		Caregiver-Reported	
		Difficulties with Parental Deployment	Reintegration Concerns	Youth's Difficulties with Deployment	Youth's Difficulties with Reintegration
Interaction between return from deployment during year before study period and time of data collection	Return & time=0	0.18 (0.25)	0.05 (0.25)	0.07 (0.28)	−0.15 (0.25)
	Return & time=1	0.08 (0.21)	0.14 (0.21)	−0.08 (0.23)	0.03 (0.21)
	Return & time=2	—	—	—	—
	No return & time=1	—	—	—	—
	No return & time=2	—	—	—	—

* .05-level F-test.

** 01-level F-test.

*** .001-level F-test.

+· .05-level *t*-test.

++ .01-level *t*-test.

+++ .001-level *t*-test.

APPENDIX E

Caregiver Tables

This appendix provides the detailed findings from the survey related to caregiver outcomes. These findings are discussed in more detail in Chapter Four. Numbers in parentheses are standard deviations.

Table E.1
Caregiver Outcomes

		Caregiver-Reported			
		Hassles with Household Responsibilities	**Hassles with Relationship with Spouse/Partner**	**Hassles with Youth Behavior, Parenting**	**Report of Own Emotional Well-Being**
Intercept		9.28 (1.33)+++	4 (0.77)+++	3.89 (0.74)+++	3.84 (1.11)+++
Data-collection phase (time)	Baseline (0)	0.95 (0.18)+++***	−0.02 (0.1)***	0.51 (0.1)+++***	0.28 (0.15)*
	First follow-up (1)	0.01 (0.18)***	−0.21 (0.1)+***	0.25 (0.1)++***	0.15 (0.15)*
	Second follow-up (2)	—	—	—	—
Military Characteristics					
Deployed parent rank	Junior enlisted (E1–E4)	0.59 (0.48)	0.42 (0.28)*	0.43 (0.26)	1.3 (0.4)+++*
	Mid-grade enlisted	0.52 (0.26)+	0.45 (0.15)++*	0.15 (0.14)	0.25 (0.22)*
	Officer (O/W)	0.15 (0.28)	0.23 (0.16)*	0.06 (0.15)	0.14 (0.23)*
	Senior enlisted (E7–E9)	—	—	—	—
Deployed parent branch	Air Force	−0.46 (0.35)	−0.01 (0.2)	−0.13 (0.19)	−0.75 (0.29)+
	Army	−0.81 (0.32)+	0.11 (0.19)	−0.27 (0.18)	−0.47 (0.27)
	Marines	−0.62 (0.53)	0.27 (0.3)	−0.13 (0.29)	−0.38 (0.44)
	Navy	—	—	—	—
Deployed parent component	Active	−1.15 (0.24)+++***	−0.44 (0.14)++***	−0.19 (0.13)	−0.93 (0.2)+++***
	Reserve/ National Guard	—	—	—	—

Table E.1—Continued

		Caregiver-Reported			
		Hassles with Household Responsibilities	Hassles with Relationship with Spouse/Partner	Hassles with Youth Behavior, Parenting	Report of Own Emotional Well-Being
Youth and Caregiver Characteristics					
Race	Multiracial/ other	0.18 (0.34)	0.31 (0.2)	0.27 (0.19)	0.41 (0.28)
	Black, non–Hispanic	0 (0.35)	0.08 (0.2)	0.13 (0.19)	−0.48 (0.3)
	Hispanic	−0.49 (0.47)	0.39 (0.27)	−0.11 (0.26)	0.32 (0.39)
	White, non-Hispanic	—	—	—	—
Youth age		0.02 (0.07)	0.02 (0.04)	0.01 (0.04)	0.08 (0.06)
Youth gender	Female	−0.21 (0.2)	−0.1 (0.12)	−0.73 (0.11)+++***	−0.11 (0.17)
	Male	—	—	—	—
Operation Purple® attendance	Yes	−0.05 (0.24)	−0.21 (0.14)	−0.06 (0.13)	0.05 (0.2)
	No	—	—	—	—
Caregiver–youth communication quality (caregiver report)		0.18 (0.04)+++***	0.04 (0.02)	0.26 (0.02)+++***	0.34 (0.03)+++***
Caregiver age		−0.01 (0.02)	0.01 (0.01)	0.01 (0.01)	−0.02 (0.02)
Caregiver gender	Female	0.94 (0.47)+ *	0.04 (0.28)	0.42 (0.26)	0.92 (0.4)+*
	Male	—	—	—	—
Caregiver employed	Employed outside home	0.81 (0.16)+++***	0.15 (0.09)	0.17 (0.09)	−0.18 (0.14)
	Not employed outside home	—	—	—	—
Caregiver education	BA or more	0.78 (0.23)+++***	0 (0.13)	0.17 (0.13)	−0.37 (0.19)
	HS degree or less	−0.69 (0.31)+***	−0.04 (0.18)	0.12 (0.17)	−0.04 (0.26)
	Some college/2-yr degree	—	—	—	—
Caregiver report of own emotional well-being (MHI-5)		0.47 (0.02)+++***	0.23 (0.01)+++***	0.14 (0.01)+++***	—

Table E.1—Continued

		Caregiver-Reported			
		Hassles with Household Responsibilities	Hassles with Relationship with Spouse/Partner	Hassles with Youth Behavior, Parenting	Report of Own Emotional Well-Being
Housing	Military (on- or off-base)	−0.33 (0.29)	−0.47 (0.16)++*	0 (0.16)	−0.55 (0.25)+*
	Own home	0.04 (0.25)	−0.29 (0.14)+*	0.06 (0.14)	−0.49 (0.22)+*
	Rent, with family, or other	—	—	—	—
Deployment Experience					
Real-time deployment flag		0.13 (0.2)	−0.36 (0.11)+++***	−0.14 (0.11)	0.57 (0.17)+++***
Deployed during study period	Yes	0.17 (0.44)	0.25 (0.25)	−0.37 (0.24)**	−0.39 (0.37)
	No	—	—	—	—
Returned during study period	Yes	−0.05 (0.46)	−0.05 (0.26)	0.05 (0.26)	1.08 (0.39)++***
	No	—	—	—	—
Deployed during year before study period	Yes	−0.17 (0.43)	−0.23 (0.25)	−0.25 (0.24)	−0.05 (0.36)
	No	—	—	—	—
Returned from deployment during year before study period	Yes	0.61 (0.32)	0.25 (0.18)	−0.1 (0.18)	0.26 (0.27)
	No	—	—	—	—
Months deployed during year before study period		0.01 (0.04)	0.03 (0.02)	0.04 (0.02)	−0.03 (0.03)
Months deployed (2001 to baseline)	1–12 months	−0.12 (0.41)	0.21 (0.24)	−0.32 (0.23)	0.13 (0.34)
	13+ months	0.37 (0.46)	0.43 (0.27)	−0.04 (0.26)	0.24 (0.39)
	Never	—	—	—	—
Total number of deployments (2001 to baseline)		0.1 (0.09)	0.01 (0.05)	0.03 (0.05)	0.02 (0.07)
Deployment location	At least one deployment in Iraq/Afghanistan	0.25 (0.28)	−0.2 (0.16)	0.26 (0.15)	0.34 (0.23)

Table E.1—Continued

		Caregiver-Reported			
		Hassles with Household Responsibilities	Hassles with Relationship with Spouse/Partner	Hassles with Youth Behavior, Parenting	Report of Own Emotional Well-Being
	No deployment in Iraq/ Afghanistan	—	—	—	—
Interaction between deployment during year before study period and time of data collection	Deploy & time=0	−0.2 (0.41)	−0.6 (0.23)++*	−0.26 (0.23)	−0.17 (0.35)
	Deploy & time=1	0.28 (0.38)	−0.23 (0.21)*	−0.09 (0.21)	0.23 (0.33)
	Deploy & time=2	—	—	—	—
	No deploy & time=0	—	—	—	—
	No deploy & time=1	—	—	—	—
	No deploy & time=2	—	—	—	—
Interaction between return from deployment during year before study period and time of data collection	Return & time=0	−0.11 (0.5)	0.33 (0.28)	0.13 (0.27)	0.36 (0.43)
	Return & time=1	0.22 (0.41)	0.09 (0.23)	0.12 (0.23)	−0.14 (0.35)
	Return & time=2	—	—	—	—
	No return & time=0	—	—	—	—
	No return & time=1	—	—	—	—
	No return & time=2	—	—	—	—

* .05-level F-test.

** 01-level F-test.

*** .001-level F-test.

+. .05-level *t*-test.

++ .01-level *t*-test.

+++ .001-level *t*-test.

Table E.2
Caregiver Deployment Outcomes

		Caregiver-Reported		
		Caregiver Concerns During Deployment (e.g., parenting)	Caregiver Concerns About Lack of Community/Social Support During Deployment	Caregiver Concerns with Deployed Parent Reintegration
Intercept		2.25 (0.42)+++	−0.01 (0.44)	1.25 (0.79)
Data-collection phase (time)	Baseline (0)	0.37 (0.06)+++***	0.25 (0.06)+++*	0.14 (0.1)*
	First follow-up (1)	−0.12 (0.11)***	0.2 (0.11)*	0.1 (0.18)*
	Second follow-up (2)	—	—	—
Military Characteristics				
Deployed parent rank	Junior enlisted (E1–E4)	0 (0.15)	0.1 (0.16)	−0.1 (0.3)
	Mid-grade enlisted	0.03 (0.08)	0.07 (0.08)	0.18 (0.15)
	Officer (O/W)	0.07 (0.09)	0.19 (0.09)+	0.09 (0.16)
	Senior enlisted (E7–E9)	—	—	—
Deployed parent branch	Air Force	−0.02 (0.11)	0.09 (0.11)	0.19 (0.21)
	Army	−0.09 (0.1)	−0.06 (0.1)	0.04 (0.19)
	Marines	−0.02 (0.16)	0.12 (0.17)	0.36 (0.31)
	Navy	—	—	—
Deployed parent component	Active	−0.06 (0.08)	−0.42 (0.08)+++***	−0.44 (0.14)++**
	Reserve/ National Guard	—	—	—
Youth and Caregiver Characteristics				
Race	Multiracial/ other	0.01 (0.1)	0.15 (0.11)	0.29 (0.2)
	Black, non-Hispanic	0.05 (0.11)	−0.01 (0.12)	0.18 (0.21)
	Hispanic	0.07 (0.15)	0.07 (0.15)	0.05 (0.28)
	White, non-Hispanic	—	—	—
Youth age		−0.04 (0.02)	0.05 (0.02)+*	0.05 (0.04)

Table E.2—Continued

		Caregiver-Reported		
		Caregiver Concerns During Deployment (e.g., parenting)	Caregiver Concerns About Lack of Community/Social Support During Deployment	Caregiver Concerns with Deployed Parent Reintegration
Youth gender	Female	−0.2 (0.06)+++***	−0.06 (0.06)	−0.11 (0.12)
	Male	0 (0)	0 (0)	0 (0)
Operation Purple® Attendance	Yes	−0.14 (0.07)	−0.02 (0.08)	−0.18 (0.14)
	No	—	—	—
Caregiver age		0.01 (0.01)	0 (0.01)	−0.01 (0.01)
Caregiver gender	Female	−0.03 (0.15)	0.09 (0.16)	0.68 (0.3)+*
	Male	—	—	—
Caregiver employed	Employed outside home	0.04 (0.06)	−0.02 (0.06)	0.2 (0.1)+*
	Not employed outside home	—	—	—
Caregiver education	BA or more	0.04 (0.07)*	0.09 (0.07)	0.04 (0.14)
	HS degree or less	0.28 (0.1)++*	0.02 (0.1)	0.07 (0.18)
	Some college/ 2-yr. degree	—	—	—
Caregiver report of own emotional well-being (MHI-5)		0.06 (0.01)+++***	0.08 (0.01)+++***	0.15 (0.01)+++***
Housing	Military (on- or off-base)	0.17 (0.1)**	−0.36 (0.1)+++***	0.08 (0.17)
	Own home	0.3 (0.09)+++**	−0.08 (0.09)***	0.06 (0.15)
	Rent, with family, or other	—	—	—
Deployment Experience				
Real-time deployment flag		−0.26 (0.07)+++***	−0.01 (0.07)	−0.2 (0.11)
Deployed during year before study period	Yes	0.1 (0.14)	0.2 (0.14)	0.15 (0.26)
	No	—	—	—
Returned from deployment during year before study period	Yes	−0.15 (0.14)	−0.06 (0.15)	−0.24 (0.27)
	No	—	—	—

Table E.2—Continued

		Caregiver-Reported		
		Caregiver Concerns During Deployment (e.g., parenting)	Caregiver Concerns About Lack of Community/Social Support During Deployment	Caregiver Concerns with Deployed Parent Reintegration
Deployed during year before study period	Yes	0.06 (0.13)	−0.13 (0.13)	−0.5 (0.25)+*
	No	—	—	—
Returned from deployment during year before study period	Yes	−0.11 (0.1)	0.14 (0.1)	0.28 (0.18)
	No	—	—	—
Months deployed during year before study period		0.02 (0.01)	0.01 (0.01)	0.03 (0.02)
Months deployed (2001 to baseline)	1–12 months	0.03 (0.13)	0.35 (0.14)+***	0.33 (0.26)***
	13+ months	0.15 (0.15)	0.6 (0.16)+++***	0.99 (0.29)+++***
	Never	—	—	—
Total number of deployments (2001 to baseline)		0.01 (0.03)	0.01 (0.03)	0.02 (0.05)
Deployment location	At least one deployment in Iraq/ Afghanistan	0.05 (0.09)	−0.17 (0.09)+*	0.11 (0.16)
	No deployment in Iraq/ Afghanistan	—	—	—
Interaction between deployment during year before study period and time of data collection	Deploy & time=0	0 (0.14)	−0.29 (0.14)+*	0.02 (0.23)
	Deploy & time=1	0.05 (0.16)	−0.44 (0.16)++*	−0.22 (0.28)
	Deploy & time=2	—	—	—
	No deploy & time=0	—	—	—
	No deploy & time=1	—	—	—
	No deploy & time=2	—	—	—

Table E.2—Continued

		Caregiver-Reported		
		Caregiver Concerns During Deployment (e.g., parenting)	**Caregiver Concerns About Lack of Community/Social Support During Deployment**	Caregiver Concerns with Deployed Parent Reintegration
Interaction between return from deployment during year before study period and time of data collection	Return & time=0	−0.05 (0.17)	0.1 (0.17)	0.19 (0.28)
	Return & time=1	0.18 (0.14)	0.23 (0.14)	0.2 (0.24)
	Return & time=2	—	—	—
	No return & time=0	—	—	—
	No return & time=1	—	—	—
	No return & time=2	—	—	—

* .05-level F-test.

** 01-level F-test.

*** .001-level F-test.

+. .05-level *t*-test.

++ .01-level *t*-test.

+++ .001-level *t*-test.

APPENDIX F

Program Participant Recommendations

This appendix summarizes program recommendations offered directly by study participants. In the surveys, we queried caregivers about programs needed for military families and also about advice they would provide other caregivers experiencing deployment. We coded these open-ended responses into categories using qualitative methods described earlier; however, we did not attempt to assess the feasibility or effectiveness of these recommendations.

Caregiver Perspectives on Program Needs

We asked caregivers to recommend areas in need of program development or additional programs. In this section, we provide the primary categories for their recommendations (see Figure F.1), and where possible, we also provide subcategories that could be collapsed and enumerated. For each recommendation area, we provide exemplar quotes.

Easier access to counseling (40 percent). Of those who responded with concerns in this area, 23 percent requested more counseling for youth, 18 percent wanted better access to counseling for those youth not living near a military installation, and 18 percent requested more family-based counseling.

Figure F.1
Caregiver Recommendations for Programs

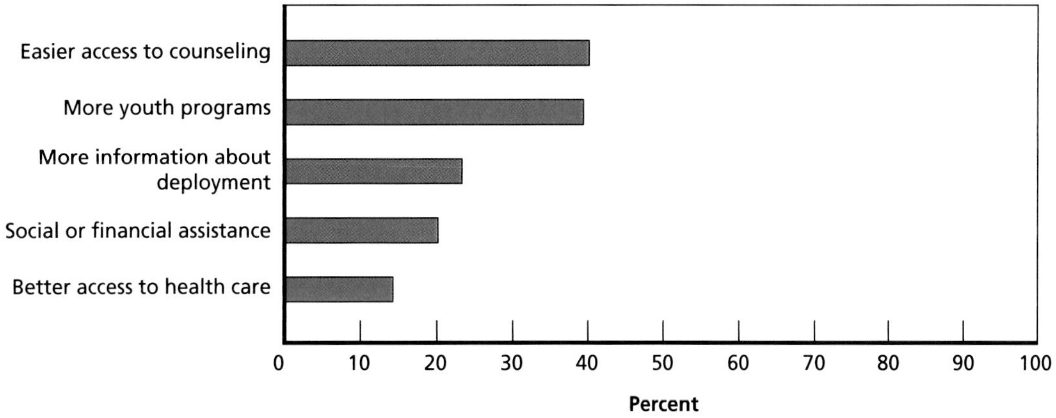

NOTE: Percentages are not mutually exclusive.
RAND *TR913-F.1*

> I think they should have predeployment counseling for families. There are households that have never experienced deployment . . . they need to know that is hard for the families. Make the counseling mandatory since there are households that won't want to go.

More programs for youth (39 percent). Of those who recommended ideas in this area, 60 percent wanted programs for youth in the form of day or weekend retreats. The remaining group requested local programs, particularly for those who did not live near an installation (11 percent).

> It would be nice if they had mini types of *Operation Purple®* camps, like all-day or weekend things, just with people from different areas, and maybe even services available for parents. Being able to do things with people geographically that are in the military, not just branch wise.

More information/resources about deployment and services available (23 percent). In general, requests for more information were unspecified, but 26 percent of those who cited a recommendation in this category requested more information from the unit, and 21 percent wanted easier access to military families (or better ways to connect).

> I'd like to get more information about the base that I'm moving to before I get there. It's hard to figure out who to ask.

Social, financial assistance (20 percent). Among these respondents, 22 percent requested more support for childcare, and 22 percent requested more financial help.

> I work in the summer and the kids don't have school, and I can't afford childcare. There should be a reduced rate for deployed spouses. There needs to be a program with housing situation to assist spouses of deployed servicemen. They're robbing the solders with their housing prices. They need to make sure officials are not overcharging the service member or their spouse.

Better access to health care in general (14 percent). Requests for better access were general, but among those who cited these types of recommendations, 41 percent wanted better access to doctors.

> When we arrived here (new post), the nearest doctor for specific things was 2 hours away. There aren't enough doctors on post. You lose prescription privileges and other things if you go off post. It would be easier if they would work with you if you go off post.

Advice for Other Caregivers

In addition to these types of recommendations for programs and services, caregivers also were asked to provide their advice to other caregivers experiencing deployment. Figure F.2 summarizes types of advice.

Support network (33 percent). This included asking for and accepting help, and maintaining connections with friends and family.

Figure F.2
Caregiver Advice for Other Caregivers

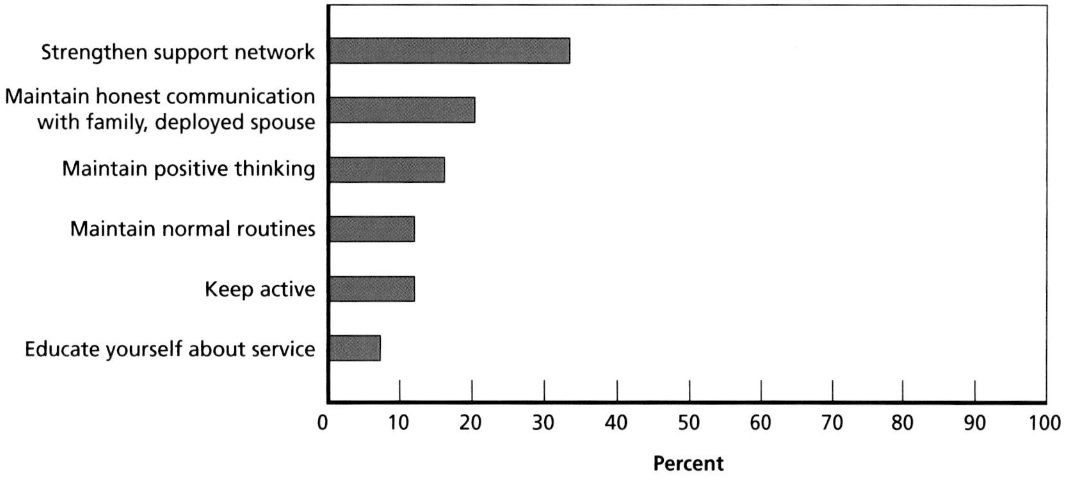

NOTE: Percentages are not mutually exclusive.
RAND *TR913-F.2*

Communication (20 percent). This included maintaining communication with deployed spouse/partner, and communicating and being honest with youth.

Perspectives/positive thinking (16 percent). Responses in this category included being patient and staying positive, being flexible, and taking life one day at a time.

Maintenance of routines (12 percent). Maintaining normal routines, keeping religious practices going, and taking care of oneself (e.g., getting sleep).

*Maintaining activity level (*12 percent). This includes staying busy and keeping youth occupied.

Preparation/education (7 percent). This included educating oneself about military procedures and taking ownership of decisions in the household.

Youth Perspectives on Program Needs

Youth also had ideas about program needs for other youth their age. This included the following:

Increased availability of youth programs (54 percent). Of those who cited ideas in this category, 47 percent requested more day or weekend camp opportunities for youth, 21 percent requested more sports-related activities, and the rest asked for general programming or arts programs.

More counseling (17 percent). Youth also cited interest in more counseling programs, and most of these respondents (85 percent) simply requested more counseling programs for youth.

Other items requested by youth included help to stay positive (13 percent), help connecting with other military youth (8 percent), and help to stay better connected with the deployed parent (4 percent).

References

American Psychological Association Presidential Task Force on Military Deployment Services for Youth, Families, and Servicemembers. "The psychological needs of U.S. military servicemembers and their families: A preliminary report." American Psychological Association, 2007. As of July 20, 2009: http://www.apa.org/about/governance/council/policy/military-deployment-services.pdf

Andrade L, Caraveo-Anduaga JJ, Berglund P, et al. "Cross-national comparisons of the prevalences and correlates of mental disorders." *Bulletin of the World Health Organization,* 2000, 78: 413–426.

Angrist JD, Johnson JH. "Effects of work-related absences on families: Evidence from the Gulf War." *Industrial and Labor Relations Review,* 2000, 54(1): 41–58.

Barker LH, Barry K. "Developmental issues impacting military families with young children during single and multiple deployments." *Military Medicine,* 2009, 174(10): 1033–1040.

Benjamin R, Costello E, Warren M. "Anxiety disorders in a pediatric sample." *Journal of Anxiety Disorders*, 1990, 4(4): 293–316.

Berwick DM, Murphy JM, Goldman PA, Ware JE, Barsky AJ, Weinstein MC. "Performance of a five-item mental health screening test." *Medical Care, 1991,* 29(2): 169–176.

Birmaher B, Brent D, Chiappetta L, et al. "Psychometric properties of the Screen for Child Anxiety Related Emotional Difficulties (SCARED): A replication study." *Journal of the American Academy of Child & Adolescent Psychiatry*, 1999, 38(10): 1230–1236.

Burrell LM, Adams GA, Durand DB, Castro CA. "The impact of military lifestyle demands on well-being, Army, and family outcomes." *Armed Forces and Society,* 2006, 33(1): 43–58.

Caplan HL, Cogall SR, Alexandra H, Robson KM. "Maternal depression and the emotional development of the child." *British Journal of Psychiatry*, 1989, 154: 818–826.

Castaneda L, Harrell M, Varda D, Hall K, Beckett M, Stern S. *Deployment Experiences of Guard and Reserve Families.* Santa Monica, Calif.: RAND Corporation, MG-645-OSD, 2008. As of November 11, 2010: http://www.rand.org/pubs/monographs/MG645/

Chandra A, Burns R, Tanielian T, Jaycox L, Scott M. "Understanding the impact of deployment on children and families. Findings from a pilot study of *Operation Purple* Camp participants." Santa Monica, Calif.: RAND Corporation, WR-566, 2008. As of November 11, 2010: http://www.rand.org/pubs/working_papers/WR566/

Chandra A, Lara-Cinisomo S, Jaycox LH, Tanielian T, Burns R, Ruder T. "Children on the homefront: The experience of children from military families." *Pediatrics,* 2010a, 125(1): 13–22.

Chandra A, Martin LT, Hawkins S, Richardson A. "The impact of parental deployment on child social and emotional functioning: Perspectives of school staff." *Journal of Adolescent Health*, 2010b, 46(3): 218–223.

Chandra A, Burns RM, Jaycox L, Tanielian T. "Understanding the deployment experience for children and youth from military families." In *Risk and Resilience in U.S. Military Families.* S Wadsworth and D Riggs (eds.). New York: Springer, 2011.

Chang JJ, Halpern CT, Kaufman JS. "Maternal depressive symptoms, father's involvement, and the trajectories of child problem behaviors in a US national sample." *Archives of Pediatrics & Adolescent Medicine,* 2007, 161(7): 697–703.

Crick NR, Bigbee MA. "Relational and overt forms of peer victimization: A multi-informant approach." *Journal of Consulting and Clinical Psychology,* 1998, 66(2): 337–347.

Drummet AR, Coleman M, Cable S. "Military families under stress: Implications for family life education." *Family Relations,* 2003, 52(3): 279–287.

Eaton KM, Hoge CW, Messer SC, Whitt AA, Cabrera OA, McGurk D, et al. "Prevalence of mental health problems, treatment need, and barriers to care among primary care-seeking spouses of military service members involved in Iraq and Afghanistan deployments." *Military Medicine,* 2008, 173(11): 1051–1056.

Engel RC, Gallagher LB, Lyle, DS. "Military deployments and children's academic achievement: Evidence from Department of Defense Education Activity Schools." U.S. Military Academy, 2006.

Farrell, AD, Kung, EM, White, KS, Valois, RF. "The structure of self-reported aggression, drug use, and delinquent behaviors during early adolescence." *Journal of Clinical Child Psychology,* 2000, 29(2): 282–292.

Flake EM, Davis BE, Johnson PL, Middleton LS. "The psychosocial effects of deployment on military children." *Journal of Developmental & Behavioral Pediatrics,* 2009, 30(4): 271–278.

Gibbs DA, Martin SL, Kupper LL, Johnson RE. "Child Maltreatment in enlisted soldiers' families during combat-related deployments." *Journal of the American Medical Association,* 2007, 298(5): 8.

Goodman R. "Psychometric properties of the Strengths and Difficulties Questionnaire." *Journal of the American Academy of Child & Adolescent Psychiatry,* 2001, 40(11): 1337–1345.

Hall L, Williams CA, Greenberg RS. "Supports, stressors, and depressive symptoms in mothers of young children." *American Journal of Public Health,* 1985, 75(5): 518–521.

Hiew CC. "Separated by their work: Families with fathers living apart." *Environment and Behavior,* 1992, 24(2): 206–225.

Hillenbrand ED. "Father absence in military families." *The Family Coordinator,* 1976, 25(4): 451–458.

Hoge CW, Castro CA, Messer SC, McGurk D, Cotting DI, Koffman RL. "Combat duty in Iraq and Afghanistan, mental health problems, and barriers to care." *New England Journal of Medicine,* 2004, 351(1): 13–22.

Hosek JR, Kavanagh J, Miller L. *How Deployments Affect Service Members.* Santa Monica, Calif.: RAND Corporation, MG-432-RC, 2006. As of November 11, 2010:
http://www.rand.org/pubs/monographs/MG432/

Huebner AJ, Mancini JA. "Adjustments among adolescents in military families when a parent is deployed." Military Family Research Institute at Purdue University, 2005.

Jaycox L, Stein BD, Paddock S, Miles J, Chandra A, Meredith LS, et al. "Impact of teen depression on academic, social and physical functioning." *Pediatrics,* 2009, 124(4): 596–605.

Jensen PS, Grogan, D, Xenakis, SN, Bain, MW. "Father absence: Effects on child and maternal psychopathology." *Journal of the American Academy of Child & Adolescent Psychiatry,* 1989, 28(2): 171–175.

Jensen PS, Martin D, Watanabe H. "Children's response to parental separation during Operation Desert Storm." *Journal of the American Academy of Child & Adolescent Psychiatry,* 1996, 35(4): 433–441.

Karney BR, Crown JS. *Families Under Stress: An Assessment of Data, Theory, and Research on Marriage and Divorce in the Military.* Santa Monica, Calif.: RAND Corporation, MG-599-OSD, 2007. As of November 11, 2010:
http://www.rand.org/pubs/monographs/MG599/

Lauver, SC, Little, PM. Recruitment and retention strategies for out-of-school-time programs. *New Directions for Youth Development,* 2005: 71–89.

Lester PK, Peterson K, Reeves J, Knauss L, Glover D, Mogil C, et al. "The long war and parental combat deployment: Effects on military children and at-home spouses." *Journal of the American Academy of Adolescent and Child Psychiatry,* 2010, 49(4): 310–320.

Levai M, Kaplan S, Ackermann R, Hammock M. "The effect of father absence on the psychiatric hospitalization of Navy children." *Military Medicine,* 1995, 160(3): 104–106.

Lipari R, Winters A, Matos K, Smith J, Rock L. “Military child well-being in the face of multiple deployments.” In *Routledge Handbook of War and Society: Iraq and Afghanistan.* SC Ford and MG Ender (eds.). London: Taylor & Francis Ltd., 2010.

Loeber R, Stouthamer-Loeber M. “Development of juvenile aggression and violence: Some common misconceptions and controversies.” *American Psychologist,* 1998, 53(2): 242–259.

Loeber R, Farrington DP, Stouthamer-Loeber M, Moffitt TE, Caspi A, Lynam D. “Male mental health problems, psychopathy, and personality traits: Key findings from the first 14 years of the Pittsburgh Youth Study.” *Clinical Child and Family Psychology Review,* 2001, 4(4): 273–297.

Lyle DS. “Using military deployments and job assignments to estimate the effect of parental absences and household relocations on children’s academic achievement.” *Journal of Labor Economics,* 2006, 24(2): 32.

Mansfield AJ, Kaufman JS, Marshall SW, Gaynes BN, Morrissey JP, Engel CC. “Deployment and the use of mental health services among U.S. Army wives.” *New England Journal of Medicine,* 2010, 362(2): 101–109.

Marta E. “Parent–adolescent interactions and psychological risk in adolescents: An analysis of communication support and gender.” *Journal of Adolescence,* 1997, 20(5): 473–487.

McCabe CJ, Thomas KJ, Brazier JE, Coleman P. “Measuring the mental health status of a population: A comparison of the GHQ-12 and the SF-36 (MHI-5).” *The British Journal of Psychiatry,* 1996, 169(4): 517–521.

McCarroll JE, Ursano RJ, Liu X, Thayer LE, Newby JH, Norwood AE, et al. “Deployment and the probability of spousal aggression by U.S. Army soldiers.” *Military Medicine,* 2000, 165(1): 41–44.

McCulloch C, Searle S. *Generalized, Linear and Mixed Models.* New York: Wiley & Sons, 2001.

Miles, MB, Huberman, AM. *Qualitative Data Analysis: An Expanded Sourcebook* (2nd ed.). Thousand Oaks, Calif.: Sage, 1994.

Nice DS. “A longitudinal analysis of Navy family separation.” San Diego, Calif.: Navy Personnel Research and Development Center, 1981.

Noam, GG. Editor-in-chief’s notes: The significance of enrollment, attendance, and engagement. In GG Noam (ed). *Participation in Youth Programs: Enrollment, Attendance, and Engagement* (*New Directions for Youth Development,* No. 105, pp. 1–4). New York: Wiley & Sons, 2005.

Pisano MC. “Implications of deployed and nondeployed fathers on seventh graders’ California achievement test scores during a military crisis.” Paper presented at the Annual Meeting of the National Association of School Psychologists, 1996.

Raschmann JK, Patterson JC, Schofield GL. “A retrospective study of marital discord in pilots: The USAFSAM experience.” Brooks Air Force Base, Tex.: School of Aerospace Medicine, 1989.

Resnick MD, Bearman PS, Blum RW, Bauman KE, Harris KM, Jones J, et al. “Protecting adolescents from harm: Findings from the National Longitudinal Study on Adolescent Health.” *The Journal of the American Medical Association,* 1997, 278(10): 823–832.

Rosenthal D, Feldman S. “The influence of perceived family and personal factors in self-reported school performance of Chinese and Western high school students.” *Journal of Research on Adolescence,* 1991, 11(2): 135–154.

Rubin, D.B. “Multiple imputation after 18+ years (with discussion).” *Journal of the American Statistical Association,* 1996, 91(434): 473–489.

SAS Institute Inc. “SAS 9.1.3 Help and Documentation.” Cary, N.C.: SAS Institute Inc., 2002–2004.

SDQ, Information for researchers and professionals about the Strengths & Difficulties Questionnaires. 2009. As of November 15, 2010:
http://www.sdqinfo.org/

Schumm WR, Hemesath K, Bell DB, Palmer-Johnson CE, Elig TW. “Did Desert Storm reduce marital satisfaction among Army enlisted personnel?” *Psychological Reports,* 1996a, 78(3, Pt 2): 1241–1242.

Schumm WR, Bell DB, Knott B, Rice RE. “The perceived effect of stressors on marital satisfaction among civilian wives of enlisted soldiers deployed to Somalia for Operation Restore Hope. *Military Medicine,* 1996b, 161(10): 601–606.

Schumm WR, Bell DB, Gade PA. "Effects of a military overseas peacekeeping deployment on marital quality, satisfaction, and stability." *Psychological Reports,* 2000, 87(3, Pt 1): 815–821.

Shuli Y, Clemens R, Hongmei Y, Xiaoming L, Stanton B, Deveaux L, et al. "Youth and parental perceptions of parental monitoring and parent-adolescent communication, youth depression, and youth risk behaviors." *Social Behavior & Personality: An International Journal,* 2006, 34(10): 1297–1310.

Tanielian T, Jaycox LH, Schell T, Marshall GN, Burnam MA, Eibner C, et al. *Invisible Wounds of War: Summary and Recommendations For Addressing Psychological and Cognitive Injuries.* Santa Monica, Calif.: RAND Corporation, MG-720/1-CCF, 2008. As of November 11, 2010: http://www.rand.org/pubs/monographs/MG720.1/

Thornberry TP, Huizinga D, Loeber R. "The prevention of serious delinquency and violence: Implications from the program of research on the causes and correlates of delinquency." In *Sourcebook on Juvenile Offenders.* Washington, D.C.: U.S. Department of Justice, 1995: 213–237.

Tomforde M. *The Emotional Cycle of Deployment.* Strausberg, Germany: Bundeswehr Institute of Social Sciences, 2006.

Turner RJ, Lloyd DA. The stress process and the social distribution of depression. *Journal of Health and Social Behavior,* 1999, 40: 374–404.

U.S. Department of Health and Human Services. National Center for Health Statistics. "National Health Interview Survey." 2001.

Varni JW, Burwinkle TM, Seid M. "The PedsQL™ 4.0 as a school population health measure: Feasibility, reliability, and validity." *Quality of Life Research,* 2006, 15(2): 203–215.

Wong L, Gerras S,. "The effects of multiple deployments on army adolescents" (Abstract). Carlisle Barracks, Pa.: Army War College Strategic Studies Institute, January 2010. As of November 15, 2010: http://www.stormingmedia.us/26/2644/A264415.html

Wormuth C, Flournoy M, Henry PT, Murdock C. "The future of the National Guard and Reserves." Center for Strategic and International Studies, 2006.

Yeatman GW. "Paternal separation and the military dependent child." *Military Medicine,* 1981, 146(5): 320–322.

You S, Furlong MJ, Felix E, Sharkey JD, Tanigawa D. "Relations among school and connectedness, hope, life satisfaction, and bully victimization." *Psychology in the Schools,* 2008, 45(5): 446–460.